Abstracts of Administrations of MONTGOMERY COUNTY Pennsylvania

1822–1850

Mary Marshall Brewer

HERITAGE BOOKS
2019

HERITAGE BOOKS
AN IMPRINT OF HERITAGE BOOKS, INC.

Books, CDs, and more—Worldwide

For our listing of thousands of titles see our website
at
www.HeritageBooks.com

Published 2019 by
HERITAGE BOOKS, INC.
Publishing Division
5810 Ruatan Street
Berwyn Heights, Md. 20740

Originally published in 2005

International Standard Book Number
Paperbound: 978-1-68034-945-0

CONTENTS

INTRODUCTION

Montgomery County was formed in 1784 from part of Philadelphia County.

Previously published by Family Line Publications was *Abstracts of Montgomery County, Pennsylvania Wills & Administrations 1784-1823* which covered Wills Books 1 - 6 (through page 184). This book continues with the administrations to 1850. A companion book, *Abstracts of the Wills of Montgomery County Pennsylvania 1824-1850* is being published concurrently.

This book continues the work done under the direction of Ellwood Roberts, completed in 1911. Copies of these abstracts were made available to various libraries in Pennsylvania and microfilm copies made by the Genealogical Society of Utah (LDS).

In making these abstracts of Montgomery County wills and administrations, Ellwood Roberts dictated to a stenographer as he read the wills and administrations at the Register's Office. Later she reproduced her notes in the manner as re-copied here.

We extend our appreciation to the Genealogical Society of Pennsylvania and encourage membership in the Society currently located at 215 S. Broad St., 7th Floor, Philadelphia, PA 19107-5325. (215) 545-0391.Hours: 10 a.m. to 4 p.m., Mon. thru Wed. On line at http://www.genpa.org.

Other addresses of note:
Historical Society of Pennsylvania
1300 Locust Street
Philadelphia, PA 19107-5699

Montgomery County Archives
1880 Markley St.
Norristown, PA 19401

Historical Society of Montgomery County
1654 DeKalb Street
Norristown, PA 19401

F. Edward Wright
Lewes, Delaware
2005

Abstracts of Administrations
of
MONTGOMERY COUNTY, PENNSYLVANIA
1822-1850

CONRAD BREY, Marlborough, 25 Nov 1822, Michael Cope, adminr.

CHARLOTTE BENNETT, 10 Dec 1822, Whitman Bennett, adminr.

FRANCES BROWER, Upper Providence, 30 Nov 1822, Abraham Brower, adminr.

DAVID DOWLIN, Horsham, 4 Dec 1822, Paul Dowlin, adminr.

ELIZABETH DISMANT, Upper Providence, 31 Dec 1822, John Wilderham, adminr.

CURTIS EVANS, Providence, 4 Dec 1822, Samuel Rhoads, adminr.

HENRY FOREMAN, Hatfield, 11 Oct 1822, Henry Foreman, Henry Brant, adminrs.

JOHN FRANCIS, New Hanover, 14 Apr 1822, Henry Kerr, Philip Heebner, adminrs.

SAMUEL FREAS, Worcester, 6 Dec 1822, Catharine Freas, Samuel Freas, Joseph Freas, adminrs.

JOHN GARBER, Upper Providence, 23 Oct 1822, Jeremiah Billeu, adminr.

JOHN GEIST, 9 Dec 1822, Valentine Geist, John Geist, adminrs.

GEORGE HEIST, Gwynedd, 12 Oct 1822, John Heist, George Heist, Jacob Heist, adminrs.

JOHN HARP, Plymouth, 4 Dec 1822, John M. Potts, adminr.

JACOB HENDRICKS, Hatfield, 6 Dec 1822, Charles Hendricks, adminr.

WILLIAM HOFFMAN, Gwynedd, 25 Nov 1822, William Hoffman, Philip Hoffman, John Jacobs, adminrs.

JACOB ISETT, Upper Providence, 26 Nov 1822, Henry Isett, Isaac Isett, adminrs.

PAUL JONES, Lower Merion, 19 Feb 1822, Paul Jones, Lloyd Jones, adminrs.

PETER KEIGER, Plymouth, 25 Nov 1822, Elizabeth Keiger, Alexander Boyd, Joseph Thomas, adminrs.

CONRAD KNATZ, Douglass, 11 Dec 1822, John Knatz, Henry Knatz, adminrs.

RINARD KEELER, Limerick, 30 Oct 1822, Joseph Keeler, Conrad Keeler, adminrs.

CHARLES LUKENS, Upper Dublin, 10 Dec 1822, Tacy Lukens, John Michener, adminrs.

MICHAEL LUDWIG, 27 Dec 1822, Elizabeth Ludwig, Jacob Bechtel, adminrs.

JONATHAN LLOYD, Moreland, 2 Dec 1822, Thomas Lloyd, Samuel Lloyd, adminrs.

DANIEL MARCH, Limerick, 28 Nov 1822, Joseph Kendall, Rinard March, adminrs.

GODFREY MILLER, Whitemarsh, 11 Dec 1822, Samuel Young, John Dager, adminrs.

THOMAS MORGAN, Hatfield, 25 Nov 1822, Elizabeth Morgan, Owen Jenkins, adminrs.

MAHLON PLUMLY, Montgomery, 29 Oct 1822, Richard Plumly, adminr.

CHRISTIAN ROHR, Hatfield, 29 Nov 1822, Abraham Heckler, John Heckler, adminrs.

HARMAN REECHNER, Montgomery, 5 Dec 1822, Jacob Reechner, Peter Hill, adminrs.

PETER RICHARDS, Pottsgrove, 26 Nov 1822, Peter Richards, Jacob Miller, adminrs.

JOHN SHANER, Pottsgrove, 5 Dec 1822, Magdalena Shaner, Samuel Schnell, adminrs.

JOHN SOWER, Limerick, 11 Dec 1822, Isaac Tyson, adminr.

PHILIP SHAMBOUGH, Providence, 25 Nov 1822, Lydia Shambough, Philip Shambough, John Gillys, adminrs.

RICHARD UMSTEAD, Providence, 4 Mar 1822, Jacob Umstead, Michael Corbit, adminrs.

JACOB WISMER, Providence, 28 Oct 1822, Jacob Wismer, Henry Wismer, Christian Wismer, adminrs.

JOHN WAGNER, 29 Nov 1822, William Miller, adminr.

RICHARD WHITTON, Abington, 25 Nov 1822, Abednego Whitton, adminr.

FREDERICK ZIEBER, 4 Dec 1822, Isaac Zieber, adminr.

DAVID THOMAS, Upper Merion, 3 May 1823, John Thomas, Jacob Shainline, adminrs.

ELIZABETH ASHENFELTER, Upper Providence, 18 Nov 1823, A. Vanderslice, adminr.

JOHN ALBRIGHT, Pottsgrove, 23 Jul 1823, Jacob Albright, adminr

LEWIS ASHENFELTER, 1 Sep 1823, John Ashenfelter, A. Vanderslice, adminrs.

ANTHONY BINDER, New Hanover, 25 Apr 1823, John Knetz, Andrew Young, adminrs.

ABRAHAM BERGEY, Franconia, 28 Jul 1823, Jacob Bergey, adminr.

ELIZABETH BITTING, New Hanover, 24 Jul 1823, Joseph Bitting, adminr.

JACOB BUTTERWAX, 2 Sep 1823, Jesse Butterwax, adminr.

JOHN BOOKHAMMER, 3 Sep 1823, Elizabeth Bookhammer, Abraham Shipe, adminrs.

JACOB BECK, New Hanover, 10 Nov 1823, Eleanor Beck, Isaac Beck, adminrs.

MICHAEL BAUM, 24 Feb 1823, Samuel Johnson, adminr.

SAMUEL BEAN, Lower Providence, 27 Dec 1823, John Fry, adminr.

THOMAS BARNES, Horsham, 16 Apr 1823, Benjamin Barnes, Thomas Barnes, adminrs.

ANDREW DRAKE, Hatfield, 12 Sep 1823, Lydia Drake, adminr.

CHARLES DICKEY, Norriton, 13 Sep 1823, Lydia Dickey, adminr.

DANIEL DEAL, Plymouth, 13 Nov 1823, Mary Deal, adminr.

ISAAC DENNIS, Limerick, 15 Mar 1823, Thomas Hillburn, Jesse Hillburn, adminrs.

JOHN DAGER, Whitemarsh, 20 Oct 1823, Frederick Dager, John Dager, Jacob Dager, adminrs.

JOHN DEWEES, Lower Providence, 20 Jan 1823, Samuel Bard, adminr.

MORDECAI DAVIS, Lower Merion, 2 Apr 1823, Eleanor Davis, adminr.

PETER DECKER, Douglass, 20 Oct 1823, John Miller, adminr.

JAMES EVANS, 27 Jan 1823, James Evans, Mark Evans, adminrs.

JONATHAN EVANS, Norriton, 3 Mar 1823, Samuel Evans, Isaac Shoemaker, adminrs.

VALENTINE EPPENHEIMER, 12 Feb 1823, David Shingle, Jacob Yocum, adminrs.

HENRY FOX, Jr., Upper Providence, 31 Mar 1823, Philip Fox, John Fox, Joshua Fry, adminrs.

ISAAC FILLMAN, Upper Salford, 31 Jul 1823, John Fillman, adminr.

JOHN FREBY, New Hanover, 14 Apr 1823, Henry Kerr, Philip Heebner, adminrs.

MARY FISHER, Springfield, 28 Oct 1823, Christian Fisher, adminr.

CHARLES GEIGER, 3 Sep 1823, George Weidner, George Dengler, adminrs.

CHARLES GARBER, Marlborough, 24 Oct 1823, Henry Garber, adminr.

JOHN GRAFF, Pottsgrove, 29 Dec 1823, Samuel Graff, adminr.

JOHN GOTWALS, Upper Providence, 23 Jun 1823, Susanna Gotwals, John Hunsicker, adminrs.

PETER HUNSBERGER, Frederick, 13 Oct 1823, Abraham Hunsberger, Jacob Hunsberger, David Oberholtzer, adminrs.

ADOLPH HOFFNAGLE, Horsham, 20 Nov 1823, William Coggins, adminr.

DANIEL HOFFMAN, Upper Hanover, 28 Jul 1823, Peter Fryer, Andrew Hoffman, adminrs.

ELIZABETH HALDEMAN, 3 May 1823, Christian Haldeman, adminr.

JACOB HELLERMAN, Cheltenham, 1 Mar 1823, Robert Hellerman, adminr.

JACOB HEIST, Franconia, 2 Apr 1823, Peter Myer, adminr.

JACOB HALLMAN, Skippack, 29 Apr 1823, Henry Hallman, Jesse Hallman, adminrs.

JACOB HARMAN, Whitemarsh, 20 Oct 1823, Henry Scheetz, Conrad Ruppel, adminrs.

JACOB HARTMAN, Pottsgrove, 4 Nov 1823, George Bechtel, adminr.

MOSES HAWKINS, Moreland, 22 Jul 1823, George Pawling, adminr.

MOSES HOBSON, Limerick, 22 Nov 1823, Joseph Royer, Abel Fitzwater, adminr.

THOMAS HILLBURN, Limerick, 15 Mar 1823, Thomas Hillburn, Jesse Hillburn, adminrs.

FREDERICK ISETT, 13 Jan 1823, Henry Isett, Abraham Isett, adminrs.

JACOB JOHNSON, Skippack, 14 Feb 1823, Sarah Johnson, John Hunsicker, adminrs.

TOBIAS JOHNSON, Pottstown, 1 Oct 1823, William Himmelbright, adminr.

ADAM KOLB, Douglass, 16 Oct 1823, Henry Hoffman, Adam Trump, adminrs.

DILLMAN KOLB, Towamencin, 2 Oct 1823, Jacob Kolb, John Kolb, Henry Swartley, adminrs.

FREDERICK KOONS, Limerick, 15 Sep 1823, Abraham Koons, Samuel Graff, adminrs.

GEORGE KLINE, Whitemarsh, 7 Nov 1823, John Haney, adminr.

HENRY KOLP, Limerick, 12 Mar 1823, David Kolp, Martin Kolp, adminrs.

MICHAEL KURTZ, New Hanover, 10 Oct 1823, John Kurtz, Michael Kurtz, Matthias Kurtz, adminrs.

MOSES KEHL, Douglass, 7 Nov 1823, Anthony Kehl, adminr.

VALENTINE KURTZ, Limerick, 8 Mar 1823, John Missimer, George Boyer, adminrs.

ANNA MARIA LINSINBIGLER, 2 Apr 1823, Samuel Linsinbigler, adminr.

GEORGE LEAF, Pottstown, 21 Oct 1823, Elizabeth Leaf, adminr.

JOHN LUKENS, Horsham, 24 Oct 1823, Charles Iredell, adminr.

NATHAN LUKENS, 30 Jan 1823, Jonathan Iredell, Mary Spencer, adminrs.

PETER LEEHMAN, Lower Providence, 8 Nov 1823, Jacob Lehman, adminr.

SAMUEL LINSINBIGLER, New Hanover, 25 Oct 1823, Paul Linsinbigler, Christian Stetlz, adminrs.

ANTHONY MILLER, Hatfield, 28 Oct 1823, Abraham Miller, adminr.

JAMES MAHONEY, Lower Providence, 17 Nov 1823, George Zimmerman, adminr.

MAJOR MCDOWELL, Upper Dublin, 10 Dec 1823, Ebenezer McDowell, adminr.

MARY MULLEN, 22 Dec 1823, Enoch Supplee, adminr.

THOMAS MAJOR, Norriton, 26 Dec 1823, Matthias Brumbach, adminr.

MATTHEW NEILY, Pottsgrove, 3 Jan 1823, Catharine Neily, adminr.

MARGARET NESMITH, 14 Mar 1823, Titus Yerkes, adminr.

NASSEY NORNY, Plymouth, 11 Apr 1823, Allan Corson, adminr.

WILLIAM NEIMAN, Pottstown, 10 Mar 1823, John Neiman, adminr.

CHRISTOPHER RAZER, 3 Sep 1823, Jacob Razer, adminr.

JACOB POLEY, Upper Providence, 13 Nov 1821, Catharine Poley, John Hunsicker, adminrs.

GEORGE STEVENS, Plymouth, 19 Nov 1821, George M. Potts, adminr.

FREDERICK HUBLER, Perkiomen & Skippack, 19 Nov 1821, Henry D. Young, adminr.

REBECCA DEWEES, Springfield, 24 Nov 1821, William Johnson, adminr.

THOMAS SHEPARD, Worcester, 1 Dec 1821, Robert Shepard, adminr.

SAMUEL JARVIS, Montgomery, 4 Dec 1821, Daniel St. Clair, adminr.

AGNESS BUSBY, Whitemarsh, 15 Dec 1821, John Busby, adminr.

JACOB HUBER, Douglass, 24 Dec 1821, Michael Huber, Jacob Huber, adminrs.

PHILIP KRICKBAUM, Lower Merion, 27 Dec 1821, Samuel Powell, adminr.

JOHN KOPLIN, Potts Grove, 1 Jan 1822, John Moser, adminr.

HESTER SHOEMAKER, Plymouth, 2 Jan 1822, John Shoemaker, David Meredith, adminrs.

JOHN HUGHES, Towamencin, 7 Jan 1822, Sarah Hughes, Enos Lukens, adminrs.

ABRAHAM BENNER, Franconia, 9 Jan 1822, Abraham Benner, Christian Benner, adminrs.

EVAN WILLIAMS, Upper Dublin, 20 Jan 1822, Joseph Houpt, adminr.

JACOB BICKLE, New Hanover, 15 Jan 1822, Jacob Bickle, Ludwick Bickle, adminrs.

RICHARD DAVIS, Pottstown, 24 Jan 1822, Mary Davis, William Tawess, adminrs.

JOHN STROUD, Norriton, 29 Jan 1822, William Stroud, adminr.

THOMAS BARBIN, Cheltenham, 29 Jan 1822, Catharine Barbin, adminr.

JOHN REIMER, Frederick, 4 Feb 1822, Jacob Schwenk, David Schwenk, Henry Schwenk, adminrs.

WILLIAM TAYLOR, Whitpain, 7 Feb 1822, Susanna Taylor, adminr.

JOHN EVANS, Upper Providence, 27 Feb 1822, Robert Evans, adminr.

JOHN FRICK, Douglass, 1 Mar 1822, George Erb, adminr.

FRANCIS HOOVER, Worcester, 1 Mar 1822, John Heiser, adminr.

PETER BISBING, Whitpain, 2 Mar 1822, Peter Bisbing, John Heist, adminrs.

JACOB MAULSBERGER, Potts Grove, 13 Mar 1822, John Maulsberger, Aaron Maulsberger, adminrs.

JAMES HAMER, Upper Providence, 20 Mar 1822, Sarah Hamer, Jesse Hamer, Charles Hamer, adminrs.

JOHN MOORE, Upper Merion, 26 Mar 1822, John Moore, Samuel Moore, Charles Moore, Jonathan Moore, adminrs.

PHILIP LUDWICK, Frederick, 27 Mar 1822, Samuel Ludwick, Jacob Ludwick, adminrs.

ELIZABETH NICE, New Hanover, 1 Apr 1822, George Nice, adminr.

LYDIA WARCH, Frederick, 1 May 1822, Philip Warch, adminr.

LAURENCE LUDENBURGH, Montgomery, 3 May 1822, Evan Jones, adminr.

WILLIAM BAKEWELL, Lower Providence, 13 May 1822, John Lee, adminr.

ALEXANDER JENNINGS, Plymouth, 14 May 1822, John Mann, adminr.

SAMUEL DAVIS, Plymouth, 29 May 1822, Mary Davis, Daniel Deal, Jr., adminrs.

THOMAS HUMPHREY, Lower Merion, 3 Jun 1822, Thomas Humphrey, adminr.

ANDREW DRAKE, Montgomery, 6 Jun 1822, Thomas Humphrey, adminr.

JOHN HENTZ, Whitmarsh, 11 Jun 1822, John Hentz, William Burke, adminrs.

JESSE LUKENS, Upper Dublin, 15 Jun 1822, Eleanor Lukens, Joseph Kenderdine, adminrs.

SAMUEL MESSIMER, Pottstown, 17 Jun 1822, Ruth Messimer, James E. Messimer, adminrs.

WILLIAM SPARE, 21 Jun 1822, Jonas Spare, adminr.

WILLIAM YOCUM, Montgomery, 22 Jun 1822, Nathan Harrar, adminr.

THOMAS WEBSTER, Abington, 29 Jun 1822, Hannah Webster, adminr.

MICHAEL RODEN, Upper Dublin, 4 Jul 1822, Jacob Fitzwater, Thomas Buckman, adminrs.

SUSANNA REES, Upper Merion, 11 Jul 1822, Jonathan Engles, adminr.

WILLIAM SHEPHARD, Plymouth, 27 Jul 1822, David Lukens, Enos Tolan, Levi Evans, adminrs.

JACOB HEYSER, Sr., Skippack, 9 Aug 1822, Jacob Hallman, Cornelius Tyson, Jacob Heyser, adminrs.

THOMAS SHOEMAKER, Upper Dublin, 12 Aug 1822, John Thomson, Eleanor Shoemaker, adminrs.

JESSE SELSER, Montgomery, 13 Aug 1822, Isaac Selser, John Neavel, adminrs.

HENRY REYNOLDS, Horsham, 19 Aug 1822, Hiram McNeils, adminr.

JONATHAN GILBERT, Upper Dublin, 21 Aug 1822, Ann Gilbert, Jesse Gilbert, adminrs.

JOHN W. RABB, Horsham, 21 Aug 1822, Senica Lukens, adminr.

JONATHAN PAUL, Whitpain, 22 Aug 1822, Isaac Ellis, John Heist, adminrs.

CHRISTIAN FRYER, New Hanover, 25 Aug 1822, Henry Royer, adminr.

JOHN KUSER, Potts Grove, 24 Aug 1822, Jacob Kuser, Henry Feery, adminrs.

WALTER EVANS, Montgomery, 28 Aug 1822, Evan Evans, Jenkin Evans, adminrs.

THOMAS SHEPARD, Whitemarsh, 29 Aug 1822, John Shepard, George M. Potts, adminrs.

JOHN CONARD, Whitemarsh, 31 Aug 1822, Henry Conard, Alan W. Corson, adminrs.

FREDERICK FAVINGER, Lower Providence, 2 Sep 1822, Henry Longacker, adminr.

FREDERICK STILLWAGGON, Lower Merion, 4 Sep 1822, Margaret Stillwaggon, adminr.

MARY BOORSE, Lower Salford, 7 Sep 1822, John S. Boorse, Jacob Kulp, adminrs.

ELIZABETH LLOYD, Moreland, 14 Sep 1822, Charles Spencer, adminr.

JOHN SNARE, Hatfield, 18 Sep 1822, William Snare, adminr.

ALEXANDER PHILIP, Lower Providence, 23 Sep 1822, Alice Philip, Benjamin Davis, Francis Burnside, adminrs.

GEORGE REIFF, Lower Providence, 26 Sep 1822, Margaret Reiff, Daniel Morgan, adminrs.

AMOS DUFFIELD, Moreland, 27 Sep 1822, Thomas W. Duffield, adminr.

JACOB LEVERGOOD, Pottsgrove, 30 Sep 1822, Eve Levergood, John Levergood, adminrs.

BENJAMIN HUGHES, Plymouth, 1 Oct 1822, Mary Hughes, Daniel Davis, adminrs.

AMOS GRIFFITH, Gwynedd, 2 Oct 1822, Thomas Shoemaker, adminr.

JACOB ROSHON, 4 Oct 1822, Anna Roshon, Philip Roshon, adminrs.

CHRISTOPHER RITTENHOUSE, 5 Oct 1822, Henry Rittenhouse, William Hamill, adminrs.

ELIZABETH CUSTER, Skippack, 5 Oct 1822, Paul Custer, adminr.

ELIZABETH PARKER, Potts Grove, 10 Oct 1822, John Hagy, adminr.

ABRAHAM MOYER, Upper Salford, 11 Oct 1822, Martin Fritz, Samuel Morgan, adminrs.

GEORGE HENVIS, Whitemarsh, 4 Oct 1824, William Henvis, adminr.

MARY ANN RUTTER, Pottstown, 7 Oct 1824, Clement S. Rutter, adminr.

ALICE THOMAS, Upper Dublin, 8 Oct 1824, Daniel Thomas, Isaac Thomas, adminrs.

JOHN ZIEGLER, Frederick, 16 Oct 1824, Ditman Ziegler, adminr.

ISAAC WOOD, Whitemarsh, 18 Oct 1824, Jonathan Wood, Samuel Maulsby, adminrs.

JOHN RAWN, Perkiomen & Skippack, 19 Oct 1824, George Rawn, Daniel Rawn, adminrs.

ISAAC MOYER, Franconia, 19 Oct 1824, Isaac Moyer, Peter Moyer, adminrs.

ALEXANDER KENNEDY, Upper Merion, 20 Oct 1824, Margaret Kennedy, William Kennedy, David R. Kennedy, adminrs.

SAMUEL DAVIS, Whitemarsh, 29 Oct 1824, Rachel H. Davis, adminr.

ENOCH MORGAN, Gwynedd, 30 Oct 1824, Isaac Kenderdine, Enoch Kenderdine, John Morgan, adminrs.

CHRISTIAN MILLER, Upper Providence, 3 Nov 1824, Christian Miller, James Miller, adminrs.

DR. JOSEPH FIELD, Limerick, 11 Nov 1824, Benjamin Field, adminr.

GEORGE KEYSER, Potts Grove, 13 Nov 1824, Eve Keyser, Jacob Keyser, adminrs.

CHRISTIAN ROSENBERGER, Lower Providence, 15 Nov 1824, Elizabeth Rosenberger, David Rosenberger, John Rosenberger, adminrs.

HUGH ROOSE, 17 Nov 1824, Daniel Davis, adminr.

JOSHUA NOTE, Lower Merion, 20 Nov 1824, Ann Note, Abraham Jones, adminrs.

BARBARA DOTTERER, Douglass, 22 Nov 1824, Berney Honitter, adminr.

ABRAHAM CLYMER, Lower Salford, 22 Nov 1824, Sarah Clymer, Daniel Boorse, adminrs.

CATHARINE EVANS, Limerick, 25 Nov 1824, Mordecai Evans, adminr.

SEPTIMUS COATES, Upper Merion, 25 Nov 1824, Rachel Coates, Samuel Coates, adminrs.

BARBARA LONG, Douglass, 2 Dec 1824, George Long, adminr.

MARY HATFIELD, Potts Grove, 9 Dec 1824, Christian Hatfield, adminr.

JOHN BENDER, New Hanover, 14 Dec 1824, John Bender, Jacob Bender, adminrs.

MICHAEL DOTTERER, Limerick, 14 Dec 1824, Margaret Dotterer, Mark Yerger, adminrs.

CATHARINE STAUFFER, Skippack & Perkiomen, 16 Dec 1824, Henry Kolb, Abraham Zeigler, adminrs.

ENCOH M. SPENCER, Upper Dublin, 18 Dec 1824, Issacher Kenderdine, adminr.

BARBARA PROTSMAN, Upper Providence, 20 Dec 1824, Peter Keyser, adminr.

CHRISTIAN SEASER, Whitemarsh, 8 Jan 1825, Henry Cook, John Slingloff, adminrs.

JACOB BEINS, Moreland, 19 Jan 1825, Thomas Borleau, adminr.

JAMES SANDS, Potts Grove, 9 Feb 1825, Frederica Spencer, adminr.

HANNAH THOMAS, Norriton, 15 Feb 1825, William Thomas.

MARY JOHNSON, Montgomery, 23 Feb 1825, Jesse Johnson, adminr.

DANIEL HAWBERGER, Marlborough, 25 Feb 1825, John Hawberger, adminr.

HARRIET RAMBO, Upper Merion, 28 Feb 1825, Aaron Rambo, adminr.

MATTHIAS TYSON, Skippack & Perkiomen, 16 Mar 1825, Benjamin Tyson, adminr.

JOHN VANDERFLIT, Whitemarsh, 17 Mar 1825, Barbara Vanderflit, adminr.

MARY BROOK, Limerick, 26 Mar 1825, Robert Brook adminr.

JELLIS KOLB, Skippack, 28 Mar 1825, John Kolb, Joseph Kolb, adminrs.

SARAH YEAKLE, Towamencin, 5 Apr 1825, Abraham Yeakle, adminr.

JOHN ROBERTS, Norriton, 9 Apr 1825, Samuel Thomas, adminr.

MARTIN KOLB, Skippack & Perkiomen, 15 Apr 1825, Jacob Hunsicker, Abraham Kolb, Dilman Kolb, adminrs.

JOHN CHILDS, Norriton, 16 Apr 1825, Jacob Moore, adminr.

JOHN BOULTON, Limerick, 19 Apr 1825, John Barlow, adminr.

JOHN AMBLER, Gwynedd, 3 May 1825, Samuel Ambler, adminr.

THOMAS KENSEY, Potts Grove, 18 May 1825, Jesse Kline, adminr.

SAMUEL HOMES, Horsham, 11 Jun 1825, Martha Homes, adminr.

RACHEL KLAIR, Whitpain, 11 Jun 1825, John Grenewalt, adminr.

SAMUEL BARD, 5 Jul 1825, Ezekiel Bard, adminr.

GEORGE EVANS, Montgomery, 25 Jul 1825, Samuel Evans, adminr.

SAMUEL EVANS, Limerick, 2 Aug 1825, Jesse Evans, adminr.

ABRAHAM YERGER, New Hanover, 6 Aug 1825, Conrad Yerger, Samuel Yerger, adminrs.

GEORGE DUNNET, Upper Dublin, 11 Aug 1825, Priscilla Dunnet, John Dunnet, Benjamin Dunnet, adminrs.

CHRISTIAN RUTH, Hatfield, 20 Aug 1825, Isaac Richert, adminr.

JACOB SCHWENK, Gwynedd, 20 Aug 1825, William Schwenk, Jacob Schwenk, Peter Summers, adminrs.

CREMONA MONTIOR, 15 Aug 1825, Joseph Montior, adminr.

JACOB GROW, Lower Merion, 22 Aug 1825, Sarah Grove, Jacob Latch, adminrs.

ABIGAIL OVERHOLTZER, Hatfield, 21 Aug 1825, John Overholtzer, adminr.

ELIZABETH ADAMS, Upper Merion, 1 Sep 1825, John B. Adams, adminr.

CHRISTIAN LIGHTCAP, Gwynedd, 10 Sep 1825, Margaret Lightcap, Jacob Hoover, adminrs.

JACOB WEBSTER, Abington, 16 Sep 1825, Sarah Ann Webster, Benjamin Webster, adminrs.

ISAAC WILLIAMS, Jr., Whitemarsh, 28 Sep 1825, Joseph Williams, Samuel Paul, adminrs.

MARY PATTERSON, Pottstown, 28 Sep 1825, Jacob Shuler, adminr.

PHILIP NYCE, Upper Salford, 1 Oct 1825, Abraham Nyce, Abraham Clemmer, adminrs.

GEORGE BOLTON LOWENS, Jr., Upper Merion, 3 Oct 1825, Mary P. Lowens, adminr.

SAMUEL ZUBER, Douglass, 8 Oct 1825, Henry Zuber, adminr.

ABRAHAM CASSELL, Worcester, 24 Oct 1825, George Cassell, adminr.

HUGH COUSTY, Upper Providence, 25 Oct 1825, Catharine Cousty, John Cousty, adminr.

WILLIAM DUNGAN, Horsham, 25 Oct 1825, Jonannah Dungan, adminr.

REBECCA PRICE, Lower Merion, 27 Oct 1825, Rees Price, adminr.

DANIEL BLYLER, Whitemarsh, 1 Nov 1825, David Blyler, Henry Daub, adminr.

GEORGE NETZ, Upper Providence, 3 Nov 1825, Jacob Custer, adminr.

RICHARD LAKE, 10 Nov 1825, Wendel Fisher, adminr.

JOHN MCCLAY, Springfield, 15 Nov 1825, Mary McClay, Jacob Nace, adminrs.

HANNAH BARNET, Upper Providence, 15 Nov, 1825, Samuel Horning, adminr.

HENRY DENGLER, New Hanover, 21 Nov 1825, Henry Schneider, adminr.

LAURENCE, TREXLER, Montgomery, 21 Nov 1825, Joseph Jarrett, adminr.

CATHARINE BLOOM, Montgomery, 21 Nov 1825, Joseph Jarret, adminr.

CHRISTIANA HYDAY, Montgomery, 21 Nov 1825, Joseph Jarrett, adminr.

JACOB SMITH, Norriton, 29 Nov 1825, Abraham Schrack, adminr.

JACOB HOFFMAN, Jr., Norriton, 5 Dec 1825, Barbara Hoffman, Jacob Hoffman, adminrs.

JACOB SCHRACK, Montgomery, 7 Dec 1825, Lewis Schrack, adminr.

ABRAHAM KLARE, Jr., Whitpain, 12 Dec 1825, Isaac Klare, adminr.

BARBARA WISLER, 17 Dec 1825, Jacob Wisler, adminr.

JOB KRIEBLER, Gwynedd, 17 Dec 1825, George Anders, Andrew Krieble, adminrs.

DAVID SCHRACK, 17 Dec 1825, John Schrack, John Shearer, adminrs.

THOMAS WILLIAMS, Cheltenham, 22 Dec 1825, Harriett A. Williams, adminr.

GEORGE HEIST, Gwynedd, 29 Dec 1825, Elizabeth Heist, John Heist, adminrs.

ABRAHAM KLINE, Frederick, 3 Jan 1826, Samuel March, adminr.

LEONARD HENDRICKS, Lower Salford, 6 Jan 1826, George Delp, adminr.

JESSE JOHNSON, 11 Jan 1826, Andrew Evans, adminr.

ISRAEL HOXWORTH, Hatfield, 20 Jan 1826, Benjamin Lee, adminr.

WILLIAM BARTLESON, Plymouth, 23 Jan 1826, Jane Bartleson, adminr.

NATHAN EVANS, Gwynedd, 7 Feb 1826, Ann Evans, John H. Cavender, adminrs.

ISSACHAR M. RHOADS, Worcester, 8 Feb 1826, Enos Lukens, John Jenkins, adminrs.

PETER BELSON, Upper Merion, 10 Feb 1826, Andrew Shainline, adminr.

JOSEPH STOVER, Hatfield, 15 Feb 1826, Jacob Stover, Henry Stover, adminrs.

JACOB REIFF, Jr., Lower Salford, 21 Feb 1826, John Reiff, Henry Kulp, Jr., adminrs.

ALICE CRAFT, Abington, 21 Feb 1826, Daniel Craft, adminr.

HENRY GROW, Lower Merion, 24 Feb 1826, Mary Grow, Joseph Smith, adminrs.

JACOB CASSEL, Hatfield, 28 Feb 1826, John Drake, adminr.

JACOB SLOUGH, Norriton, 1 Mar 1826, Jacob Slough, Matthias Brumback, adminrs.

WILLIAM CROLE, Frederick, 6 Mar 1826, Jonathan Jones, adminr.

CHARLES J. WAGNER, Upper Merion, 9 Mar 1826, John Wagner, adminr.

JOHN NEWEL, Moreland, 10 Mar 1826, Joseph Warner, Jonathan Duboir, adminrs.

ELIZABETH LONGBINE, Limerick, 13 Mar 1826, George Longbine, adminr.

DEBORAH AYRES, Moreland, 13 Mar 1826, James Comly, adminr.

JESSE STALL, Jefferson Co, 14 Mar 1826, John Rhoads, adminr.

SAMUEL MANN, Horsham, 15 Mar 1826, Isaac Mann, adminr.

DIANA N. CLINCH, Norristown, 17 Mar 1826, Charles Jones, adminr.

JOHN REIFF, Lower Salford, 17 Mar 1826, Abraham Ruth, adminr.

ABRAHAM DUFFIELD, Whitpain, 31 Mar 1826, Richard Duffield, adminr.

ANDREW YOUNG, Marlborough, 3 Apr 1826, John Young, Andrew Young, adminrs.

MARY TYSON, Upper Providence, 8 Apr 1826, Robert Tyson, adminr.

ANDREW BOYER, Upper Providence, 20 Apr 1826, John Todd, adminr.

MARIA MARGARET HAWBERGER, Potts Grove, 17 Apr 1826, Peter Hawberger, adminr.

CHARLES BISSON, Worcester, 18 Apr 1826, John Bisson, adminr.

ROBERT E. HOBART, Potts Grove, 29 Apr 1826, Nathaniel O. Hobart, adminr.

MARGARET BURK, Upper Dublin, 9 May 1826, James Gilkeson, adminr.

NICHOLAS STYER, Upper Hanover, 16 May 1826, Jacob Styer, Henry Styer, adminrs.

THOMAS R. CRAIG, Norriton, 20 May 1826, William Hamill, adminr.

SUSANNA JONES, Lower Merion, 23 May 1826, Griffith Jones, adminr.

CYRESS CADWALDER, Abington, 5 Jun 1826, James Paul, adminr.

ABRAHAM TYSON, Lower Providence, 7 Jun 1826, William Tyson, adminr.

DAVID LONGACRE, Upper Providence, 15 Jun 1826, John Longacre, Christopher Longacre, Daniel Longacre, adminrs.

JOHN BRIGHT, Upper Dublin, 15 Jun 1826, Jonathan Bright, Edward Bright, adminrs.

SAMUEL DANA, Norristown, 19 Jun 1826, William Morrison, adminr.

EPHRAIM FENTON, Cheltenham, 23 Jun 1826, Samuel Fenton, James Fenton, adminrs.

ADAM BEAN, Gwynedd, 24 Jun 1826, Samuel Bean, John Selser, adminrs.

JOSEPH WHITCOMB, Upper Dublin, 10 Jul 1826, Catharine Whitcomb, Henry Daub, adminrs.

GEORGE NYCE, Marlborough, 5 Aug 1826, John Miller, Samuel Miller, adminrs.

JACOB MATTIS, Plymouth, 26 Aug 1826, Eleanor Mattis, Amos Mattis, Benjamin Mattis, adminrs.

JOHN PLUCK, Norriton, 28 Aug 1826, Thomas Read, adminr.

MALACHA FISHER, Upper Dublin, 4 Sep 1826, Abraham Fisher, adminr.

ANDREW HAINS, Franconia, 5 Sep 1826, Henry Barnt, Andrew Hains, adminrs.

JOHN HORN, Lower Merion, 11 Sep 1826, Elizabeth Horn, George Horn, adminrs.

JOHN WIERMAN, Skippack & Perkiomen, 21 Sep 1826, George Hawk, George Slotterer, adminrs.

JACOB GEHMAN, Franconia, 29 Sep 1826, Abraham Swartley, Samuel Gehman, adminrs.

JOHN ANDREW, Whitemarsh, 9 Oct 1826, Adam Kitler, Sr., adminr.

SAMUEL WENTZ, Whitpain, 10 Oct 1826, Isaac Ellis, adminr.

ARCHIBALD MAGUIRE, Whitemarsh, 18 Oct 1826, George Martis, Alan W. Corson, adminrs.

HANNAH BROOKE, Limerick, 18 Oct 1826, William Towers, adminr.

ABRAHAM SILFUS, Upper Providence, 21 Oct 1826, Abraham Keeley, adminr.

JOB SPENCER, Moreland, 23 Oct 1826, Edward Spencer, adminr.

JONATHAN MATSON, Lower Merion, 23 Oct 1826, Isaac Dehaven, Joseph Crawford, adminrs.

CHRISTIAN HEFFLEFINGER, Limerick, 26 Oct 1826, Jacob Hefflefinger, adminr.

JOHN ZIMMERMAN, Lower Providence, 26 Oct 1826, Henry Custer, adminr.

LEWIS T. MILLER, Skippack, 13 Oct 1826, Benjamin T. Miller, adminr.

JACOB FOX, Potts Grove, 30 Oct 1826, Samuel Schnell, adminr.

GEORGE LONGBINE, Limerick, 31 Oct 1826, George Longbine, Abraham Poll, adminrs.

MARY ROBERTS, Abington, 4 Nov 1826, George Brooks, adminr.

ELIZABETH HART, Plymouth, 8 Nov 1826, Jacob Hart, Jr., George Tippen, adminrs.

JACOB WAGNER, Lower Salford, 10 Nov 1826, Michael Wagner, Joseph Groff, adminrs.

SARAH RICHARDS, New Hanover, 16 Nov 1826, George D. Richards, Jacob Smith, adminrs.

HENRY LANDES, Skippack & Perkiomen, 20 Nov 1826, Jacob Landes, Henry Swardley, adminrs.

PHILIP REIMER, Frederick, 20 Nov 1826, Margaret Reimer, Samuel Kepler, adminrs.

ATKINSON FARRA, Norriton, 1 Dec 1826, Samuel Lukens, David Jarrett, adminrs.

MAHLON BRADFIELD, Abington, 7 Dec 1826, Anna Bradfield, Abner Bradfield, adminrs.

CHARLES ROBERTS, Lower Merion, 8 Dec 1826, Richard Roberts, adminr.

ANNA YOCUM, Franconia, 20 Dec 1826, James Yocum, adminr.

JOHN WHITPAIN, Lower Merion, 19 Dec 1826, John Whitman, Jacob Bailer, adminrs.

JACOB HOMAN, Pottstown, 27 Dec 1826, Andrew Eckert, adminr.

DAVID ZELL, Lower Merion, 29 Dec 1826, John Matheys, adminr.

MARY PHILLIPS, Upper Merion, 6 Jan 1827, Samuel Philips, adminr.

JOHN DOWNING, Pottstown, 11 Jan 1827, Henry Schneider, adminr.

ELIZABETH JACK, Pottstown, 16 Jan 1827, William Towers, adminr.

PATRICK MULLEN, Whitpain, 22 Jan 1827, Catharine Mullen, adminr.

CHARLOTTE TYSON, Abington, 25 Jan 1827, Joshua Tyson, adminr.

HENRY MILLER, Potts Grove, 31 Jan 1827, Henry Lessig, adminr.

FRANCIS HUGHES, Lower Providence, 8 Feb 1827, Susannah Hughes, adminr.

CHRISTOPHER ZIMMERMAN, Worcester, 9 Feb 1827, Arnold S. Zimmerman, William Zimmerman, adminrs.

MARTIN FRITZ, Potts Grove, 20 Feb 1827, Peter Fritz, Jr., Peter Fritz, Sr., adminrs.

ABRAHAM HARPER, Norristown, 15 Feb 1827, Ann Harper, William Powell, adminrs.

RACHEL BARNES, Moreland, 20 Feb 1827, Nathaniel B. Boileau, adminr.

JACOB LEWIS, Limerick, 22 Feb 1827, William Towers, adminr.

JACOB MOYER, Upper Salford, 26 Feb 1827, Henry Moyer, John Moyer, adminrs.

PATIENCE MORGAN, Lower Merion, 26 Feb 1827, Joseph C. Morgan, adminr.

CLARINDER FISHER, Moreland, 3 Mar 1827, John Walker, adminr.

JOHN FRANTZ, Whitpain, 5 Mar 1827, Catharine Frantz, adminr.

GREGORY SCHULTZ, Upper Hanover, 6 Mar 1827, Daniel Schultz, David Yeakle, adminrs.

FREDERICK WANNER, Norriton, 10 Mar 1827, John Wanner, Jacob Wanner, Henry Beaver, adminrs.

CHRISTIAN BERGEY, Franconia, 14 Mar 1827, John Bergey, Henry Berndt, adminr.

ISABELLA CRAWFORD, 16 Mar 1827, Andrew Crawford, Hugh Crawford, adminrs.

HENRY ROTH, New Hanover, 19 Mar 1827, Daniel Hock, adminr.

HANNAH RYAL, 23 Mar 1827, Henry Ryal, adminr.

CATHARINE TIPPIN, Plymouth, 24 Mar 1827, George Tippin, adminr.

HENRY NEYMAN, Potts Grove, 16 Apr 1827, Jacob Keyser, David Neyman, adminrs.

HENRY BERGEY, Franconia, 5 May 1827, Elizabeth Bergey, Isaac Bergey, adminrs.

JOHN BROMLY, Lower Merion, 8 May 1827, Mary Bromly, adminr.

JOHN EASTBURN, Upper Merion, 12 May 1827, Isaac Eastburn, Benjamin Eastburn, adminrs.

JOHN KNOX, Upper Providence, 25 May 1827, Andrew Knox, adminr.

JAMES KNOX, Norriton, 25 May 1827, Andrew Knox, adminr.

JESSE FRONEFIELD, Lower Providence, 25 May 1827, John Fronefield, adminr.

ISAAC KIRK, Upper Dublin, 30 May 1827, John Kirk, adminr.

ISAAC WYNKOOP, Moreland 12 Jun 1827, Isaac Van Cleve, adminr.

JOHN HOMSHER, Worcester, 30 Jun 1827, Catharine Homsher, Jesse Homsher, adminrs.

CONRAD GEIST, New Hanover, 14 Jul 1827, Maria Geist, Daniel Geist, Henry Geist, adminrs.

SAMUEL CONARD, Norristown, 2 Aug 1827, Sarah Conard, adminr.

JOHN FETTER, Norristown, 6 Aug 1827, Matthias Fetter, adminr.

RACHEL CLIME, Whitpain, 9 Aug 1827, Collom Clime, adminr.

EZEKIEL WOOD, Whitpain, 11 Aug 1827, John Ryle, adminr.

JOHN WILSON, Norristown, 13 Aug 1827, George Wertzner, adminr.

FREDERICK CONRAD, Norristown, 16 Aug 1827, Catharine Conrad, Frederick Conrad, Philip Hoover, adminrs.

DANIEL COOK, Upper Merion, 22 Aug 1827, Alexander Cook James Cook, adminrs.

JOHN WEAK, Horsham, 23 Aug 1827, Morgan Morgan, Jr., adminr.

WILLIAM RIGHTER, Lower Merion, 27 Aug 1827, Joseph Righter, William Fisher, adminrs.

ABRAHAM REIFF, Upper Providence, 28 Aug 1827, Joseph Reiff, Abraham Brown, adminrs.

HENRY LEISTER, 12 Sep 1827, Michael Leister, Philip Leister, adminrs.

HOMER DUBRE, Gwynedd, 17 Sep 1827, Lewis Warner, Morgan Morgan, adminrs.

JOHN BAKER, Norristown, 20 Sep 1827, Thomas Miller, adminr.

CONRAD FAGELY, Douglass, 21 Sep 1827, Jacob Fagely, John Fagely, Daniel Miller, adminrs.

GEORGE JAGS, Marlborough, 24 Sep 1827, Joseph Geiger, adminr.

CHRISTOPHER HEEBNER, 27 Sep 1827, Hannah Heebner, David Heebner, adminrs.

WILLIAM PRICE, Lower Providence, 27 Sep 1827, Henry Hallman, George Snyder, adminrs.

MARY HALLMAN, Skippack & Perkiomen, 27 Sep 1827, Henry Hallman, George Snyder, adminrs.

PETER BENNER, Hatfield, 29 Sep 1827, Owen Jenkins, adminr.

ANDREW FISHER, Whitemarsh, 5 Oct 1827, John Fisher, Andrew Fisher, George Fisher, adminrs.

PETER YOST, Potts Grove, 10 Oct 1827, Daniel Yost, Jacob Yost, John Hendricks, adminrs.

DAVID DAVIS, Plymouth, 11 Oct 1827, Charlotte Davis, adminr.

SOPHIA GEIGER, Whitemarsh, 15 Oct 1827, John Righter, adminr.

SIMON FREAS, Whitemarsh, 24 Oct 1827, William Freas, Charles Freas, John Dager, adminrs.

VALENTINE NUNGESSER, Lower Providence, 31 Oct 1827, Christian Detwiler, adminr.

ISAIAH PAXSON, Abington, 1 Nov 1827, Elizabeth Paxson, adminr.

PETER HARTENSTINE, 6 Nov 1827, Samuel Schrack, adminr.

BARNEY BISBING, Horsham, 8 Nov 1827, Dorothy Bisbing, John Bisbing, adminrs.

SEBASTIAN BENNER, Franconia, 20 Nov 1827, Abraham Benner, Isaac Benner, adminrs.

JACOB SNYDER, Worcester, 20 Nov 1827, Jacob Rosenberger, John Casselberry, adminrs.

WILLIAM MEGARGE, Cheltenham, 19 Nov 1827, Isaac Hellerman, adminr.

ADAM NEIDIG, New Hanover, 20 Nov 1827, Henry Neidig, Daniel Miller, adminrs.

BARBARA AAGERMAN, Horsham, 20 Nov 1827, Wilhilmers Corson, adminr.

RUTH HUTSEL, Potts Grove, 20 Nov 1827, James Evans, adminr.

ABRAHAM BECHTLE, Upper Hanover, 22 Nov 1827, Anna Bechtel, Abraham Hunsberger, adminrs.

JACOB RASOR, Upper Providence, 26 Nov 1827, Michael Rasor, adminr.

ABRAHAM STAUFFER, Marlborough, 29 Nov 1827, Esther Stauffer, Henry Stauffer, adminrs.

MORRIS STEPHENS, Upper Merion, 6 Dec 1827, William Stephens, William Richardson, adminrs.

LYDIA WENTZ, Whitemarsh, 10 Dec 1827, Jonathan Wentz, Jacob Wentz, adminrs.

MARY SPENCER, Upper Dublin, 10 Dec 1827, Miriam Spencer, adminr.

JOHN THOMAS, Lower Merion, 14 Dec 1827, Joseph W. Thomas, adminr.

JOHN GILLHAM, Potts Grove, 15 Dec 1827, George Zollers, adminr.

SAMUEL CONRAD, Horsham, 19 Dec 1827, Sarah Conrad, Joseph Kenderdine, adminrs.

BERNARD STREPER, Springfield, 20 Dec 1827, George Martin, Leonard Streper, adminrs.

MORDECAI WILLETS, Norristown, 31 Dec 1827, Thomas Lowry, adminr.

GEORGE BECKTEL, Potts Grove, 1 Jan 1828, George Bechtel, adminr.

JOHN HARNER, Whitemarsh, 3 Jan 1828, Joseph Harner, Henry Harner, Samuel Harner, adminrs.

VALENTINE LOCKMAN, New Hanover, 8 Jan 1828, George Burger, adminr.

MICHAEL KRICK, Marlborough, 8 Jan 1828, Philip Zepp, adminr.

JACOB WUNDERLICK, Marlborough, 8 Jan 1828, Philip Rudy, George Wunderlick, adminrs.

EZEKIEL BARD, Norriton, 10 Jan 1828, John Shannon, adminr.

SAMUEL BARD, Upper Hanover, 21 Jan 1828, George Cran, adminr.

JOHN ALTHOUSE, Franconia, 22 Jan 1828, George Schwenck, Tobias Schole, adminrs.

LEWIS PENNAL, Upper Merion, 23 Jan 1828, Joseph Pennal, adminr.

JACOB STYER, 28 Jan 1828, Joseph Jones, Charlotte Jones, adminrs.

JAMES TINNA, Upper Dublin, 31 Jan 1828, James Tinna, adminr.

JOHN COATES, Norristown, 8 Feb 1828, Dedimia Coates, adminr.

HENRY REES, Hatfield, 25 Feb 1828, Jacob Rees, adminr.

JONATHAN LATE, 27 Feb 1828, Alexander Ramsey, adminr.

JACOB HILLEGAS, Upper Hanover, 3 Mar 1828, Charles Hillegas, Jacob Hillegas, Adam Kline, adminrs.

JOSEPH OVERHOLTZER, Hatfield, 4 Mar 1828, Henry Overholtzer, Jacob Ruth, adminrs.

ABRAHAM ESBACH, Douglass, 10 Mar 1828, Christian Esbach, David Esbach, adminrs.

JACOB GILBERT, Whitemarsh, 17 Mar 1828, Jacob Gilbert, Daniel Gilbert, adminrs.

ABNER STAPLETON, Norristown, 19 Mar 1828, Deborah Stapleton, adminr.

WILLIAM JEANES, Moreland, 19 Mar 1828, Isaac Jeanes, Isaiah Jeanes, adminrs.

CATHARINE STALE, Upper Providence, 22 Mar 1828, John Getty, adminr.

ROBERT HELLERMAN, Cheltenham, 26 Mar 1828, Martha Hellerman, adminr.

MICHAEL HORLOCKER, New Hanover, 14 Apr 1828, Conrad Brey, John Horlocker, adminrs.

PETER WALT, Limerick, 14 Apr 1828, Jacob Swenck, adminr.

JACOB ACHUFF, Abington, 22 Apr 1828, Eleazor Hallowell, adminr.

WILLIAM HAWKINS, Moreland, 25 Apr 1828, James Hawkins, adminr.

ELIZABETH GERHARD, Worcester, 26 Apr 1828, George Schultz, Anthony S. Heebner, adminr.

HENRY SCHNEIDER, Whitpain, 7 May 1828, Elizabeth Schneider, adminr.

CHARLES GEIGER, Potts Grove, -- May 1828, Jacob Geiger, Jonas Geiger, adminrs.

MARY KIRK, Upper Dublin, 5 Jun 1828, Isaac Tyson, John Childs, adminrs.

WILLIAM BROADES, Lower Merion, 26 Jun 1828, George Pechin, adminr.

HENRY H. GROFF, Whitpain, 30 Jun 1828, John Heist, Isaac Ellis, adminrs.

BARBARA REIFF, Upper Providence, 1 Jul 1828, Abraham Brower, adminr.

JOHN BEAN, Worcester, 19 Jul 1828, Henry Bean, Peter Bean, adminrs.

DENNIS CONRAD, Abington, 31 Jul 1828, George C. Conrad, Samuel Scholfield, adminrs.

JESSE FITZGERALD, Upper Providence, 7 Aug 1828, William Fitzgerald, adminr.

JOHN SHOEMAKER, Frederick, 8 Aug 1828, William Tyson, Jacob Reifsnyder, adminrs.

JONAS GEIGER, Potts Grove, 21 Aug 1828, George Zeales, adminr.

JOHN COULSTON, Plymouth, 1 Sep 1828, Catharine Coulston, adminr.

HENRY CASSEL, Skippack & Perkiomen, 6 Sep 1828, Samuel Cassel, Benjamin Cassel, adminrs.

CHARLES HOLT, Abington, 9 Sep 1828, Ann Holt, adminr.

CASPER COLER, Whitemarsh, 16 Sep 1828, Casper Schlater, Henry Dull, adminrs.

GEORGE HERR, Perkiomen & Skippack, 23 Sep 1828, Catharine Herr, David Herr, adminrs.

JOHN LIVEZEY, Cheltenham, 23 Sep 1828, Maria Livezey, Anthony Williams, adminrs.

JESSE JARRETT, Horsham, 26 Sep 1828, David Jarrett, Charles Tyson, adminrs.

WILLIAM LAWRENCE, Plymouth, 27 Sep 1828, Alan W. Corson, adminr.

ENOS BARNS, Whitemarsh, 2 Oct 1828, Joseph Barns, George Martin, adminrs.

HENRY RUTH, Worcester, 18 Aug 1823, Abraham Weigner, Henry Snyder, adminrs.

MAGDALENA RENNINGER, Upper Hanover, 10 Jun 1823, Elizabeth Gougler, adminr.

MARGARET REINSBURRY, Montgomery 17 Oct 1823, Thomas Shoemaker, Henry Storver, adminrs.

PETER REES, Pottsgrove, 22 Sep 1823, Charles Clay, adminr.

ABRAHAM SHUTT, 4 Oct 1823, John Shutt, Abraham Funk, adminrs.

CATHARINE SETTLER, 29 Aug 1823, William Stall, John Roberts, adminrs.

CONRAD SHAMEL, Montgomery, 6 Sep 1823, Emanuel Shamel, Jacob Shive, adminrs.

DAVID SHUTT, Lower Providence, 21 Jan 1823, Henry Wismer, adminr.

DANIEL STRADLING, Abington, 8 Aug 1823, William Rhoads, adminr.

DAVID SHOEMAKER, Springfield, 7 Nov 1823, Isaac Shoemaker, Henry Hallman, adminrs.

DANIEL SHELKOP, Pottsgrove, 20 Oct 1823, Abraham Shelkop, adminr.

JOSIAH SUPPLEE, 9 Jan 1823, Rachel Supplee, adminr.

JOSEPH SANDS, 12 Feb 1823, William Sands, adminr.

LEWIS SHELMIRE, 28 Jul 1823, Ajax Conrad, adminr.

WILLIAM THOMPSON, Pottstown, 14 Nov 1823, John Thompson, adminr.

HARMAN UMSTEAD, Skippack, 23 Apr 1823, Barbara Umstead, John Umstead, Jacob Umstead, Nathan Custer, adminrs.

ANDREW WALTZ, Limerick, 15 Apr 1823, Henry Waltz, Elizabeth Waltz, Samuel Schwenk, adminrs.

GERTRUDE WAMBACH, Pottsgrove, 7 Apr 1823, John Umstead, John Barton, adminrs.

GEORGE WISMER, Upper Providence, 10 May 1823, Joseph Henry, adminr.

HENRY WISHEY, Upper Salford, 13 Sep 1823, Daniel Kline, Henry Wishey, adminrs.

MARGARET WILBRAHAM, Providence, 17 Apr 1823, John Wilbraham, adminr.

MATTHIAS WENTZ, Springfield, 2 Oct 1823, Jonathan Wentz, Jacob Wentz, adminrs.

ELIZABETH CANCK, 24 Jan 1823, Susanna Barr, adminr.

HENRY ZINK, Frederick, 15 Oct 1823, Jacob Zink, Jacob Boyer, adminrs.

PHILIP ZEPP, 13 Jan 1823, Mary Zepp, Henry Zepp, Philip Zepp, adminrs.

WILLIAM ZEIGLER, Skippack & Perkiomen, 18 Aug 1823, Garret Zeigler, Abraham Zeigler, adminrs.

JOHN YOUNG, Lower Merion, 28 Jul 1823, David Young, William Stillwagon, adminrs.

JONAS YOST, Pottsgrove, 25 Apr 1823, Philip Yost, adminr.

EDWARD MORGAN, 15 Oct 1823, Thomas Adamson, adminr.

ELIZABETH MILLER, Limerick, 20 Nov 1823, Philip Roshong, adminr.

JOHN PALMER, Horsham, 7 Oct 1823, George Palmer, adminr.

JOHN PETERMAN, Limerick, 14 Nov 1823, Jacob Peterman, Francis Peterman, adminrs.

DANIEL SUTCH, Gwynedd, 5 Aug 1823, William Davis, adminr.

JOHN SMITH, Gwynedd, 15 Feb 1823, Adam Smith, John Griffin, adminrs.

JOHN SAHLOR, Limerick, 7 Apr 1823, John Royer, adminr.

JACOB SMITH, Upper Salford, 11 Aug 1823, Frederick Smith, Jacob Kline, adminr.

JONATHAN SHAW, Abington, 25 Aug 1823, David Thomas, adminr.

JOHN SLICHTER, Limerick, 23 Oct 1823, John Slichter, Jacob Slichter, John Freedley, adminr.

ISAAC TYSON, Skippack, 26 Mar 1823, Barbara Tyson, John Tyson, adminrs.

JOHN TYSON, 23 Sep 1823, Abraham Tyson, William Tyson, adminrs.

JOSHUA TAYLOR, Abington, 26 Dec 1823, William Grant, adminr.

JESSE TYSON, Lower Providence, 31 Dec 1823, Maria Tyson, Abraham Brower, adminrs.

MARY THOMAS, Lower Merion, 13 Aug 1823, Jacob Bealer, adminr.

JOSEPH WRIGHT, Horsham, 22 Oct 1823, Jacob Wright, Thomas Wright, adminrs.

HENRY ALTHOUSE, Franconia, 19 Jan 1824, Jacob Althouse, Benjamin Reiff, adminrs.

EZRA BARTLESON, 16 Nov 1824, Mary Bartleson, adminr.

ELIZABETH BARTOLET, 27 Jan 1824, John Bartolet, adminr.

JESSE BARNES, Whitpain, 9 Mar 1824, Hester Barnes, Edward Evans, adminrs.

JACOB BEAN, Perkiomen & Skippack, 10 May 1824, Joseph Bean, Henry Hartel, John Hendricks, adminrs.

JOHN BUSH, Whitpain, 21 May 1824, Mary Bush, Samuel Bush, James Bush, adminrs.

SARAH BROOKE, Limerick, 8 Apr 1824, William Brooke, adminr.

THOMAS BOYD, Douglass, 21 Jan 1824, Mary Boyd, Copeland Boyd, adminrs.

HENRY DONE, Limerick, 19 Apr 1824, Catharine Bone, Israel Burns, adminrs.

JOHN DE HAVEN, Upper Merion, 31 Apr 1824, Hannah DeHaven, adminr.

JACOB DAUB, Upper Salford, 9 Apr 1824, Jacob Daub, Solomon Artman, adminrs.

THOMAS DAVIS Providence, 5 Aug 1824, Samuel Davis, Philip Davis, Daniel Davis, adminrs.

ALEXANDER EHL, 9 Feb 1824, John Ehl, Daniel Ehl, adminrs.

JACOB FUNK, Lower Providence, 17 Jan 1824, Mary Funk, Christian Detwiler, adminrs.

JACOB FLECK, Gwynedd, 7 Apr 1824, Henry Hallman, Mary Fleck, Jacob Danehower, adminrs.

MARY FITZWATER, Upper Dublin, 27 Oct 1824, Joshua Tyson, adminr.

MARY FREED, Skippack & Perkiomen, 10 Jul 1824, Jacob Landes, Jacob Kulp, adminrs.

DAVID GETTY, Upper Providence, 15 Jan 1824, Robert Getty, adminrs.

JACOB GROFF, Upper Salford, 17 Feb 1824, Joseph Groff, John Groff, adminrs.

ABRAHAM HEISTANT, Upper Hanover, 31 Mar 1824, Jacob Heistant, Abraham Heistant, adminrs.

JACOB HORNING, Skippack, 12 Jan 1824, Jesse Horning, Nathan Horning, adminrs.

JOHN HEEBNER, Norriton, 26 Mar 1823, Elizabeth Heebner, Jacob Hoffman, adminrs.

MARY HATFIELD, Pottsgrove, 2 Mar 1824, Jonas Yocum, adminr.

MARY HAGEY, Whitemarsh, 9 Jun 1824, George Rex, John Hagey, adminrs.

PETER HONNATER, Pottsgrove, 12 Apr 1824, Berney Honnater, Matthias Yergey, adminrs.

COESER ISHMAEL, New Hanover, 19 Jan 1824, Samuel Ishmael, adminr.

WILLIAM JOHNSON, Perkiomen & Skippack, 11 Mar 1824, Jacob Keyser, adminr.

HUGH LLOYD, Horsham, 30 Jan 1824, David Lloyd, adminr.

SAMUEL LANDIS, Lower Providence, 13 Apr 1824, Hannah Landis, Jacob Hunsicker, adminrs.

MARY OSBORN, Whitpain, 1 Mar 1824, Nathan Osborn, adminr.

ENOS ROBERTS, Gwynedd, 16 Aug 1824, Nathan Roberts, John Roberts, Edward Roberts, adminrs.

RUDOLPH REIGHTER, Lower Merion, 1 Mar 1823, Samuel Stern, adminr.

AARON SMITH, Lower Merion, 23 Sep 1824, John Smith, adminr.

ELIZABETH SHEPHARD, Plymouth, 20 Feb 1824, William Shephard, adminr.

ELEANOR SHOEMAKER, Upper Dublin, 10 Sep 1824, John Thompson, James Rutter, adminrs.

JOHN SPECE, Limerick, 15 Mar 1824, Mary Spece, Jacob Spece, adminrs.

MICHAEL STETLER, Upper Providence, 20 Aug 1824, Elizabeth Stetler, Henry De Haven, adminrs.

JOHN WILLIAMS, Upper Dublin, 31 Mar 1824, William Williams, Rowland Williams, adminrs.

BENJAMIN BRYANT, Abington, 24 Jul 1824, Richard Shoemaker, adminr.

CONRAD BINDER, New Hanover, 21 Apr 1824, Jacob Renninger, adminr.

GEORGE HEYDRICK, Upper Salford, 27 Mar 1824, Jeremiah Krieble, adminr.

WILLIAM IVES, 21 Feb 1824, Jesse Ives, adminr.

ISAAC KOLB, Upper Providence, 10 Feb 1824, Jacob Hunsicker, Jacob Rittenhouse, adminr.

JOHN QUINN, Upper Merion, 15 Jun 1824, Joseph King, adminr.

ANN RAMSEY, Plymouth, 18 Mar 1824, Alexander Ramsey, adminr.

CHARLES TERRY, Moreland, 24 Jul 1824, Sarah Terry, adminr.

JOHN TOMPKINS, 15 Mar 1824, Samuel Cadwalder, adminr.

GEORGE MOWRER, New Hanover, 10 Oct 1828, Daniel Pennebecker, Garret C. Walker, adminrs.

WILLIAM BARR, Lower Merion, 10 Oct 1828, Jane Barr, Daniel Nippes, adminrs.

PETER LEVERGOOD, New Hanover, 11 Oct 1828, Catharine Levergood, adminr.

MARY NACE, Whitemarsh, 11 Oct 1828, Daniel Nace, adminr.

PETER DENNIG, Frederick, 13 Oct 1828, Jacob Boyer, adminr.

GEORGE NYCE, New Hanover, 16 Oct 1828, Andrew Markley, Henry Pennypacker, adminrs.

HENRY SAUDER, Frederick, 17 Oct 1828, John Sauder, John Yoder, adminrs.

EBENEZER RAMBO, Upper Merion, 18 Oct 1828, Magdalena Rambo, adminr.

JOHN VAN WINKLE, 21 Oct 1828, Susannah Van Winkle, Alan W. Corson, adminrs.

JOHN FISHER, Whitemarsh, 27 Oct 1828, Margaret Fisher, John Katz, adminrs.

AARON FISHER, Abington, 28 Oct 1828, Levi Foulke, adminr.

MORRIS LLEWELLYN, Lower Merion, 28 Oct 1828, Jane Llewellyn, Ruben Vaughan, adminrs.

ROBERT THOMAS, Whitpain, 28 Oct 1828, Samuel Thomas, adminr.

ABRAHAM CASSEL, Hatfield, 29 Oct 1828, Jacob Cassel, Henry Cassel, adminrs.

JACOB HENDRICKS, Lower Salford, 30 Oct 1828, Isabella Hendricks, John Hendricks, adminrs.

CHARLES WALTER, Marlborough, 1 Nov 1828, George Walter, Jacob Walter, adminrs.

JOSEPH THOMAS, Lower Merion, 7 Nov 1828, Lewis Thomas, John Thomas, adminrs.

JACOB RAMSEY, Upper Merion, 10 Nov 1828, Lewis Ramsey, David Shupert, adminrs.

WILLIAM SHAFFER, Potts Grove, 11 Nov 1828, Jacob Shaffer, adminr.

JACOB KEMMERER, Douglass, 11 Nov 1828, Henry Kemmerer, Charles Kemmerer, adminrs.

ENOCH BEAM, Gwynedd, 13 Nov 1828, Thomas Beam, John Jenkins, adminrs.

SUSANNA HOFFMAN, Gwynedd, 13 Nov 1828, John Jenkins, adminr.

SUSANNA BARTOLET, Frederick, 15 Nov 1828, John Bartolet, Daniel Bartolet, adminrs.

PETER ARNOLD, Plymouth, 15 Nov 1828, Daniel Arnold, adminr.

FREDERICK BAKER, Norriton, 18 Nov 1828, Jesse Bean, Matthias Brumback, adminrs.

CATHARINE NUSS, Whitemarsh, 18 Nov 1828, John Righter, Frederick Nuss, adminrs.

HENRY MARKLEY, Lower Salford, 22 Nov 1828, Abraham Benner, adminr.

JAMES CARMAN, 27 Nov 1828, Sarah Carman, adminr.

JOHN CAIN, Norristown, 28 Nov 1828, George M. Potts, adminr.

JACOB BERKEY, Lower Salford, 28 Nov 1828, John Berkey, David Berkey, adminrs.

CATHARINE BENNER, Franconia, 2 Dec 1828, Abraham Benner, adminr.

ABRAHAM CASSEL, Towamencin, 20 Dec 1828, Joseph Cassel, Henry Cassel, adminrs.

WILLIAM LEWIS, Lower Merion, 23 Dec 1828, Charles Kugler, adminr.

JAMES ANDERSON, Upper Merion, 23 Dec 1828, Martha Anderson, Nathaniel M. Leonard, adminrs.

CHARLES RAMBO, Upper Merion, 27 Dec 1828, Priscilla Rambo, John Hughes, adminrs.

JOHN RONEY, Abington, 29 Dec 1828, Jonathan Lefferts, adminr.

JOHN RAMBO, Upper Merion, 8 Jan 1829, Samuel Rambo, adminr.

JONATHAN COULSTON, Norristown, 10 Jan 1829, George Govett, adminr.

JESSE HARKER, Moreland, 14 Jan 1829, John Clayton, adminr.

SAMUEL CHRISTIAN BRANDT, Plymouth, 17 Jan 1829, Jacob Alberston, adminr.

CATHARINE CAUFFMAN, Whitemarsh, 19 Jan 1829, Frances Cauffman, adminr.

SAMUEL FUNK, Cheltenham, 25 Jan 1829, David Funk, Jesse Gilbert, adminrs.

JOHN MORGAN, Lower Merion, 26 Jan 1829, Joseph C. Morgan, adminr.

JOHN GEISENGER, Upper Salford, 6 Feb 1829, Samuel Geisenger, William Slotterer, Jr., adminrs.

DANIEL OTT, Upper Dublin, 20 Feb 1829, Francis Ott, adminr.

ELIZABETH DETWILER, Whitemarsh, 17 Feb 1829, Joseph Lukens, adminr.

CASPER FETTER, Moreland, 18 Feb 1829, Thomas B. Montange, adminr.

GEORGE DEAVES, Plymouth, 19 Feb 1829, Elizabeth Deaves, adminr.

JOHN SOWER, Upper Providence, 24 Feb 1829, Joseph Sower, adminr.

JOSEPH LEWIS, Gwynedd, 25 Feb 1829, Evan Jones, Samuel Thomas, David Thomas, adminrs.

JOHN SNYDER, Limerick, 2 Mar 1829, Peter Snyder, Jacob Pennypacker, John Pennypacker, adminrs.

HESTER BOILEAU, Moreland, 9 Mar 1829, Nathaniel B. Boileau, adminr.

JACOB FRONEFIELD, Upper Providence, 4 Mar 1829, William Fronefield, Robert Evans, adminrs.

WILLIAM PERRY, Norristown, 10 Mar 1829, Risdon Perry, adminr.

JOHN HERSTINE, Limerick, 20 Mar 1829, David Herstine, adminr.

JANE POTTS, Lower Merion, 16 Mar 1829, George M. Potts, adminr.

RICHARD JARRETT, Horsham, 16 Mar 1829, Gainor Jarrett, adminr.

THOMAS EVANS, Gwynedd, 19 Mar 1829, Joseph M. Evans, adminr.

GEORGE SMITH, Potts Grove, 23 Mar 1829, John Kuntz, adminr.

SAMUEL MARKLEY, Norristown, 31 Mar 1829, John Zeiber, adminr.

BARNABY FRANCIS, Whitemarsh, 13 Apr 1829, Charles Francis, adminr.

HUMPHREY J. WHITE, Towamencin, 14 Apr 1829, Susanna White, Abraham Yeakle, adminrs.

ANN HARKER, Moreland, 8 Apr 1829, John Clayton, adminr.

WILLIAM HALLOWELL, Sr., Horsham, 20 Apr 1829, William Hallowell, adminr.

JOHN CHAIN, Norriton, 4 May 1829, Ann Chain, adminr.

SAMUEL BICKLE, New Hanover, 5 May 1829, Peter Bickle, Samuel Thomas, adminrs.

JACOB SHADE, Upper Providence, 15 May 1829, Henry Shade, adminr.

GEORGE CRESSMAN, Cheltenham, 21 May 1829, Andrew Cressman, adminr.

HENRY TROXEL, Upper Hanover, 1 Jun 1829, Samuel Troxel, Henry Roudenbush, adminrs.

ENOCH JONES, Lower Merion, 9 Jun 1829, Paul G. Jones, adminr.

HENRY KEPNER, Limerick, 19 Jun 1829, James Evans, adminr.

WILLIAM ZEIGLER, Whitpain, 8 Jul 1829, George Heilig, John Heist, adminrs.

JOSEPH RAMBO, Limerick, 9 Jul 1829, Hannah Rambo, adminr.

ABRAHAM WILLIAMS, Worcester, 17 Jul 1829, William Hendricks, adminr.

FREDERICK W. CONRAD, Norriton, 24 Jul 1829, Elizabeth Conrad, William Anslee, adminrs.

JACOB THONEY, Upper Hanover, 24 Jul 1829, Casper Shultz, Gabriel Shultz, adminrs.

ANDREW GREBER, Upper Hanover, 27 Jul 1829, Henry Greber, Jacob Gerhard, adminrs.

BARBARA CUSTER, Worcester, 27 Jul 1829, Benjamin Custer, John Cassel, adminrs.

SOPHIA MILLER, Whitpain, 6 Aug 1829, Jonah Umstead, adminr.

PETER CUSTER, Worcester, 17 Aug 1829, Benjamin Custer, adminr.

JOHN THOMAS, Montgomery, 20 Aug 1829, Gainor Thomas, John Foreman, Jacob Cassel, adminrs.

JOHN HOFFMAN, Lower Merion, 28 Aug 1829, Hannah Hoffman, adminr.

SARAH QUIMEY, Horsham, 1 Sep 1829, Joseph Hampton, adminr.

SAMUEL SLINGLUFF, Whitpain, 3 Sep 1829, Henry Slingluff, William Rhoads, adminrs.

SARAH DUNN, Horsham, 7 Sep 1829, Jesse Haner, adminr.

JOHN GERHART, Sr., Franconia, 16 Sep 1829, George H. Gerhart, Jacob Berndt, adminrs.

BALTZER EARNEST, Upper Dublin, 21 Sep 1829, William Earnest, Samuel Earnest, Christian Keisel, adminrs.

EDWARD JENKINS, Gwynedd, 28 Sep 1829, Charles Jenkins, Jesse Jenkins, adminrs.

JOHN I. HOUGH, Montgomery, 2 Oct 1829, Benjamin Hough, adminr.

ISAAC KEYSER, Worcester, 16 Oct 1829, Margaret Keyser, Paul Custer, adminrs.

DAVID YOUNG, Marlborough, 16 Oct 1829, Henry Anthony, adminr.

JACOB SNYDER, Upper Hanover, 23 Oct 1829, Catharine Snyder, Henry Snyder, adminrs.

JOHN SHUECK, Marlborough, 26 Oct 1829, Jacob Deetz, adminr.

SAMUEL DAVIS, Plymouth, 2 Nov 1829, Daniel Davis, adminr.

JANE SMITH, 3 Nov 1829, James Paul, adminr.

JONATHAN BERRELL, Cheltenham, 12 Nov 1829, William S. Berrell, adminr.

JOHN JACKSON, Upper Providence, 16 Nov 1829, Margaret Jackson, adminr.

JOHN HOXWORTH, Lower Merion, 23 Nov 1829, Elizabeth Hoxworth, Jacob Barler, adminrs.

JONAS REINWALT, Towamencin, 25 Nov 1829, Henry Snyder, Joseph Snyder, adminrs.

ISAAC DAVIS, Upper Merion, 27 Nov 1829, Anthony Kelty, adminr.

EVE LEVERGOOD, Pottstown, 8 Dec 1829, John Levergood, adminr.

JACOB HORNING, Perkiomen & Skippack, 8 Dec 1829, John Beaver, Lewis Horning, adminrs.

GUNNER RAMBO, Norristown, 10 Dec 1829, Mordecai Williams, adminr.

HENRY NEVIL, Jr., Whitpain, 15 Dec 1829, John Rile, adminr.

ABRAHAM BENNER, Lower Salford, 16 Dec 1829, John Zeber, Jacob Markley, adminrs.

JOHN THAW, 23 Dec 1829, James Pronty, adminr.

HANNAH FOULKE, Gwynedd, 24 Dec 1829, Edward Foulke, adminr.

BENJAMIN HALLOWELL, Norriton, 2 Jan 1830, George Boyer, Jonathan Hallowell, adminrs.

JOHN CAMPBELL, 7 Jan 1830, Thomas Read, adminr.

JACOB DEWEES, Whitemarsh, 8 Jan 1830, Jacob Dewees, Henry Dewees, Daniel Dewees, adminrs.

BENJAMIN HUMPHREYS, Lower Merion, 14 Jan 1830, Thomas Humphreys, adminr.

HARRY SHAID, Marlborough, 18 Jan 1830, George Shaid, adminr.

MARY ZIMMERMAN, Worcester, 18 Jan 1830, William Zimmerman, adminr.

JOSEPH REIFF, Worcester, 19 Jan 1830, George Reiff, Andrew Tyson, adminrs.

WILLIAM SANDMAN, Upper Dublin, 20 Jan 1830, Elizabeth Sandman, adminr.

GRIFFITH OWEN, Norristown, 23 Jan 1830, George Govett, adminr.

LEWIS KNOX, Lower Merion, 21 Jan 1830, Isaiah Knox, adminr.

THOMAS HALLOWELL, Upper Dublin, 8 Feb 1830, James Paul, adminr.

JACOB GROFF, Upper Salford, 8 Feb 1830, Catharine Groff, John Zeber, John Shaffer, adminrs.

MARY ROBERTS, 23 Feb 1830, Matthew Roberts, adminr.

JOHN MINTER, Upper Salford, 1 Mar 1830, Jonas Hauberger, adminr.

PETER TYSON, Upper Dublin, 1 Mar 1830, David Thomas, adminr.

WILLIAM P. THOMAS, Lower Merion, 2 Mar 1830, Tacy Thomas, Joseph W. Thomas, adminrs.

CHARLES GILL, Lower Merion, 4 Mar 1830, George W. Roberts, adminr.

FRANCIS DAVIS, Worcester, 15 Mar 1830, Christiana Davis, adminr.

PHILIP STONG, Worcester, 16 Mar 1830, Barbara Stong, Henry Stong, Philip Stong, adminrs.

CHARLES MARTIN, Gwynedd, 22 Mar 1830, Jacob Martin, adminr.

CADWALLADER FOULKE, Gwynedd, 29 Mar 1830, Franklin Foulke, Jesse Spencer, adminrs.

CHRISTIAN DONAT, Upper Dublin, 13 Mar 1830, Elizabeth Donat, Christopher Keyser, adminrs.

SUSANNA CASSEL, Worcester, 20 Apr 1830, Jacob Cassel, adminr.

ROBERT GETTY, Lower Providence, 18 Sep 1830, John Getty, Joseph Fry, adminrs.

EDWARD ELY, Moreland, 23 Sep 1830, Evan Jones, James Paul, adminrs.

FREDERICK SOLIDAY, Moreland, 20 Apr 1830, Susanna Soliday, adminr.

MORDECAI KENDIG, Upper Salford, 20 Apr 1830, John Kendig, Martin Kendig, adminrs.

HENRY ANTHONY, Lower Salford, 20 Apr 1830, Susanna Anthony, John Sell, adminrs.

CHRISTIAN GRABER, Upper Hanover, 21 Apr 1830, Henry Graber, adminr.

JOHN SCHWENK, Frederick, 5 May 1830, Jacob Schwenk, adminr.

DAVID KERBAUGH, Upper Dublin, 15 Jun 1830, Jacob Kerbaugh, Isaac Strunk, adminrs.

JOHN FULTON, Lower Providence, 21 Jun 1830, Thomas Fulton, Joseph Fulton, adminrs.

HENRY LEARNHART, Cheltenham, 28 Jun 1830, Elizabeth Learnhart, George Martin, adminrs.

GEORGE ERNHART, Frederick, 27 Jul 1830, Jacob Zepp, adminr.

JOHN HELLINGS, Plymouth, 31 Jul 1830, Margaret Hellings, John Hellings, William Hellings, adminrs.

SAMUEL LLEWELLYN, Lower Merion, 9 Aug 1830, Morris O. Llewellyn, adminr.

JACOB NICE, Upper Salford, 16 Aug 1830, Anna Nice, Abraham Nice, adminrs.

ISAAC ROSENBERGER, Hatfield, 16 Aug 1830, Jacob Rosenberger, Henry Rosenberger, Isaac Rosenberger, adminrs.

JOSEPH LEVERGOOD, Potts Grove, 16 Aug 1830, Henry Moser, adminr.

JONES YERKES, Whitemarsh, 1 Sep 1830, Ezra Comfort, adminr.

WILLIAM ZIMMERMAN, Norriton, 3 Sep 1830, David Rittenhouse, Ezekiel Rhoads, adminrs.

ROBERT M. PHILLIPS, Abington, 23 Sep 1830, William Lukens, David Thomas, adminrs.

MARY KRIEBEL, Lower Salford, 1 Oct 1830, Joseph Kriebel, adminr.

DANIEL WALTON, Moreland, 4 Oct 1830, George H. Pawling, adminr.

JOSEPH LEWIS, Whitemarsh, 15 Oct 1830, Joseph Mather, adminr.

MARTHA LUKENS, Whitemarsh, 18 Oct 1830, Joseph Lukens, adminr.

JACOB DAUB, Upper Salford, 23 Oct 1830, Solomon Artman, John Cramer, adminrs.

JULIANNA SHAINER, Potts Grove, 1 Nov 1830, Andrew Shainer, adminr.

RYNEAR TYSON, Springfield, 2 Nov 1830, Jonathan Tyson, adminr.

JOHN FREED, Sr., Franconia, 2 Nov 1830, John Freed, George Gerhart, adminrs.

SIMON KEESEY, Norristown, 9 Nov 1830, Jesse Keesey, John Keesey, adminrs.

JOHN WARNER, Worcester, 4 Nov 1830, Mary Warner, Amos Warner, Dewalt Warner, Michael Tilling, Charles Hendricks, adminrs.

FREDERICK WAMPOLE, Whitemarsh, 11 Nov 1830, Mary Wampole, Nicholas Rapine, adminrs.

CHARLES LUKENS, Upper Dublin, 16 Nov 1830, John Fitzwater, adminr.

MARGARET MANN, Horsham, 17 Nov 1830, Isaac Mann, adminr.

SILAS SAYLOR, Gwynedd, 24 Nov 1830, Jesse Spencer, adminr.

JOSEPH FOX, Upper Hanover, 26 Nov, 1830, William Fox, Michael Heebner, adminrs.

GEORGE DUNNET, Upper Dublin, 13 Nov 1830, Jacob Fisher, David George, adminrs.

DANIEL ROSENBERGER, Hatfield, 31 Dec 1830, John W. Rosenberger, John Frick, adminrs.

WILLIAM SANDS, Pottstown, 13 Jan 1831, John Miller, adminr.

ADAM HENRY, Marlborough, 6 Dec 1830, Henry Henry, adminr.

LEWIS DOLBY, Lower Merion, 8 Dec 1830, Abraham Dolby, adminr.

JOSEPH W. PRICE, Lower Merion, 14 Dec 1830, Ann E. Price, adminr.

JOSEPH A. PRICE, Lower Merion, 14 Dec 1830, Ann E. Price, adminr.

SAMUEL HARNER, Whitemarsh, 22 Dec 1830, George Martin, William Burk, adminrs.

ANN CRAWFORD, Upper Merion, 28 Dec 1830, Joseph Crawford, William Crawford, adminrs.

ELIZABETH EISENBERG, Limerick, 29 Dec 1830, John Eisenberg, adminr.

ADAM KITLER, Whitemarsh, 3 Feb 1831, Adam Kitler, adminr.

ANNA SEAF, Pottstown, 22 Jan 1831, George L. Seaf, adminr.

JOHN HARWOOD, Worcester, 27 Jan 1831, John Roberts, adminr.

MARGARET BAUGHMAN, Horsham, 28 Jan 1831, John Baughman, adminr.

JOSEPH LYSINGER, Plymouth, 3 Feb 1831, Henry Lysinger, Samuel Lysinger, adminrs.

WILLIAM WALTON, Moreland, 7 Feb 1831, Elishia Walton, adminr.

JACOB VANFOSSEN, Worcester, 9 Feb 1831, Benjamin Spare, Jesse Umstead, adminrs.

JOHN COURSEN, Limerick, 12 Jan 1831, William Coursen, adminr.

JACOB YERGER, Douglass, 14 Feb 1831, John Yerger, Jacob Yerger, adminrs.

HANNAH C. SHOEMAKER, Moreland, 14 Feb 1831, John Kenderdine, adminr.

JOHN BROADES, Lower Merion, 21 Feb 1831, John Pechin, George Pechin, adminrs.

HENRY UMSTEAD, Upper Providence, 21 Feb 1831, Isaac Price, adminr.

JOHN BOYER, Upper Salford, 1 Mar 1831, Frederick Rudy, John Drake, adminrs.

ABRAHAM KRIEBLE, Worcester, 28 Feb 1831, George Krieble, Joseph Krieble, adminrs.

GEORGE FITZWATER, Norristown, 1 Mar 1831, Rebecca Fitzwater, Charles Thomas, Merchant Maulsby, adminrs.

JOHN EMERY, Limerick, 1 Mar 1831, George Moore, adminr.

GEORGE FITZWATER, Norriton, 1 Mar 1831, Charles Thomas, Merchant Maulsby, adminrs.

EDWARD P. WALTER, Lower Merion, 10 Mar 1831, Joseph Brookfield, adminr.

WILLIAM SHAY, Horsham, 20 Mar 1831, Jonathan Shay, Thomas Shay, adminrs.

HUGH FOULKE, Gwynedd, 4 Mar 1831, Cadwallader Foulke, adminr.

RICHARD BLAUKLEY, Lower Merion, 21 Mar 1831, Anthony Blaukley, George F. Curwen, adminrs.

MARGARET GEYER, Frederick, 22 Mar 1831, George Zieber, adminr.

JONATHAN JEANES, Moreland, 22 Mar 1831, Seth Holt, adminr.

JOHN LAND, Montgomery, 23 Mar 1831, Martha Land, Jesse Hubbs, adminrs.

DERRICK KEYSER, Worcester, 24 Mar 1831, Jacob Keyser, John Johnson, adminrs.

ABRAHAM KEELEY, Upper Providence, 28 Mar 1831, Jacob Fryer, adminr.

ABRAHAM PHILIPS, Whitpain, 31 Mar 1831, Samuel Philips, William M. Glathery, adminrs.

JOSEPH ANDERS, Towamencin, 31 Mar 1831, Andrew Kriebel, Jacob Kulp, adminrs.

JACOB LINENBAUGH, Plymouth, 2 Apr 1831, Joseph Jarrett, adminr.

HENRY BERNDT, Upper Salford, 4 Apr 1831, Henry Berndt, Abraham Heaney, adminrs.

JACOB WEIDEMOYER, Marlborough, 4 Apr 1831, Elizabeth Weidemoyer, John Geyer, adminrs.

JACOB REES, Sr., Hatfield, 8 Apr 1831, Mary Rees, Phillip Rees, adminrs.

DILLMAN STAUFFER, Norriton, 15 Apr 1831, James Pennypacker, William Hamill, adminrs.

JOHN HOUPT, Upper Dublin, 19 Apr 1831, Samuel Houpt, adminr.

SAMUEL EVANS, Limerick, 20 Apr 1831, George Rambo, adminr.

GEORGE MISSIMER, Pottstown, 22 Apr 1831, Amos Missimer, Daniel Yost, adminrs.

HENRY UPDEGRAVE, Skippack & Perkiomen, 22 Apr 1831, Abraham Tyson, adminr.

SARAH PAULMIER, 25 Apr 1831, George Wilson, adminr.

JACOB ROSENBERGER, Worcester, 26 Apr 1831, John Hunsicker, Christian Detwiler, adminrs.

CHARLES MATHER, Whitpain, 2 May 1831, Jane Mather, Job R. Mather, adminrs.

MICHAEL RUTH, Gwynedd, 3 May 1831, Jacob Ruth, Abraham Moyer, adminrs.

VALENTINE SMITH, Whitemarsh, 5 May 1831, Jacob K. Smith, Benjamin Corson, adminrs.

JACOB SHRIVER, Abington, 6 May 1831, Mary Dillon, Ardemus Stewart, adminrs

ALEXANDER MOORE, Upper Merion, 7 May 1831, George M. Potts, adminr.

HANNAH DRAKE, Montgomery, 14 May 1831, Jacob Fitzwater, Evan Jones, adminrs.

WILLIAM GILBERT, Upper Dublin, 16 May 1831, Sarah Gilbert, Israel Gilbert, adminrs.

JACOB KOLP, Whitemarsh, 18 May 1831, Mary Kolp, Daniel Kolp, John Kratz, adminrs.

HENRY S. DANNEHOWER, Gwynedd, 19 May 1831, Mary Dannehower, George Weisel, Jr., adminrs.

THEODORE DUFFIELD, Whitpain, 23 May 1831, John Fitzgerald, adminr.

CATHARINE WISLER, Hatfield, 13 Jun 1831, Isaac Wisler, adminr.

JOHN WEBSTER, Moreland, 16 Jun 1831, James Paul, adminr.

JOSEPH BECHTEL, Potts Grove, 17 Jun 1831, Andrew Eskerd, adminr.

JOHN GEORGE YERGER, New Hanover, 18 Jul 1831, Peter Yerger, adminr.

JAMES WHITBY, Upper Merion, 25 July 1831, Anthony Whitby, Andrew Keiger, adminrs.

WILLIAM TENNIS, Towamencin, 27 Jul 1831, Sarah Hughes, Enos Lukens, adminrs.

WILLIAM BROADES, Lower Merion, 29 Jul 1831, George Pechin, adminr.

GEORGE ADAM BLAUCK, Upper Hanover, 2 Aug 1831, John Blauck, William Blauck, adminrs.

JOHN KIRK, Upper Dublin, 3 Aug 1831, Rebecca Kirk, John L. Kirk, adminrs.

CATHARINE MAUERER, Franconia, 15 Aug 1831, Michael Mauerer, adminr.

MARTHA HALLOWELL, Abington, 16 Aug 1831, Timothy Hallowell, David Thomas, adminrs.

JOHN LOUCKS, Lower Providence, 16 Aug 1831, Henry Loucks, adminr.

ELI KEELER, Limerick, 20 Aug 1831, Jacob Gilbert, adminr.

ENOCH SUPPLEE, Norriton, 22 Aug 1831, John Supplee, adminr.

WILLIAM SPRIGGS, Whitemarsh, 24 Aug 1831, Fuestena Spriggs, adminr.

JESSE WARNER, Skippack, 29 Aug 1831, Peter Warner, Frederick Knipe, adminrs.

HENRY BOYER, Upper Hanover, 15 Sep 1831, Henry Boyer, Jacob Boyer, adminrs.

JOHN HOCKMAN, Franconia, 20 Sep 1831, Henry Hockman, John Hockman, adminrs.

HENRY BISBING, Norriton, 20 Oct 1831, William McGlathery, adminr.

WILLIAM H. HALLOWELL, Lower Merion, 30 Oct 1831, John Hallowell, adminr.

BARNABAS MAULSBY, Jamica Island, 18 Oct 1831, John Maulsby adminr.

JOHN GROFF, Sr., Frederick, 18 Oct 1831, Christian Souder, adminr.

THOMAS POTTS, 19 Oct 1831, Joseph M. Potts, adminr.

GEORGE AIRMAN, Whitpain, 21 Oct 1831, Catharine Airman, John Shenberger, adminrs.

GEORGE LEIDY, Hatfield, 22 Oct 1831, Samuel Wambold, Frederick Rotsell, adminrs.

MICHAEL ZEIGLER, Upper Salford, 26 Oct 1831, Ann Zeigler, Jesse Zeigler, adminrs.

JOHN ZOLLER, Skippack & Perkiomen, 15 Nov 1831, Edward Zoller, John Bean, Jr., adminrs.

JOHN FULMER, Limerick, 17 Nov 1831, Jesse Hilborn, adminr.

JAMES CRAIG, Norriton, 21 Nov 1831, William Hamill, adminr.

WILLIAM HAMMAN, Plymouth, 22 Nov 1831, Hugh Crawford, adminr.

PAUL CUSTER, Whitpain, 23 Nov 1831, Nathan Lewis, adminr.

BENA EGLER, Plymouth, 3 Dec 1831, Isaac Wood, adminr.

SAMUEL DEHAVEN, Lower Merion, 8 Dec 1831, Joseph P. Dehaven, Isaac Dehaven, adminrs.

BENJAMIN ROWLAND, Cheltenham, 4 Jan 1832, Samuel Rowland, Benjamin Mather, adminrs.

JOSHUA MORRIS, Cheltenham, 6 Jan 1832, Joseph Mather, adminr.

DR. WILLIAM JOHNSON, Upper Providence, 16 Jan 1832, Sarah Johnson, adminr.

HANNAH CRESSMAN, Franconia, 16 Jan 1832, Frederick Huntsberger, adminr.

ELIZABETH BARNES, Moreland, 16 Jan 1832, Hiram Barnes, adminr.

JOHN LANDIS, Upper Providence, 17 Jan 1832, Abraham Landis, David Longacker, adminrs.

JOHN ROBINSON, Upper Dublin, 17 Jan 1832, Thomas Peine, adminr.

JOHN ROBENSON, Upper Dublin, 17 Jan 1832, Moses Prine, adminr.

LLEWELLYN J. TAYLOR, Lower Merion, 19 Jan 1832, Samuel Young, John Righter, adminrs.

ELIZABETH LYSINGER, Plymouth, 21 Jan 1832, Samuel Lysinger, adminr.

DOROTHY LAUER, 17 Feb 1832, Philip Lauer, adminr.

JACOB DAVIS, New Hanover, 17 Feb 1832, George Heiser, Henry Heiser, adminrs.

DEDEMIAH GILBERT, Cheltenham, 21 Feb 1832, Jesse Gilbert, adminr.

JAMES SPENCER, Upper Dublin, 27 Feb 1832, Spencer Shoemaker, adminr.

JONATHAN CLEAVER, Montgomery, 21 Mar 1832, Elias Cleaver, adminr.

JACOB REIFSNIDER, Frederick, 26 Mar 1832, Jesse Reifsnider, Richard Reifsnider, adminrs.

JACOB PENH, Providence, 26 Mar 1832, John Penh, adminr.

JOHN SHUTT, Lower Salford, 28 Mar 1832, Jacob Shutt, John Shutt, adminrs.

JOSEPH THOMAS, Plymouth, 29 Mar 1832, Ann Thomas, William Thomas, George M. Potts, adminrs.

MARY WALTER, Whitpain, 31 Mar 1832, George Walter, adminr.

DANIEL P. IREDELL, Horsham, 31 Mar 1832, John Iredell, Jr.

DAVID CROLL, Upper Hanover, 2 Apr 1832, Catharine Croll, Jacob Schwench, adminrs.

WILLIAM SPENCER, Upper Dublin, 9 Apr 1832, Lydia D. Spencer, Charles Thomas, adminrs.

HENRY STILL, Whitpain, 9 Apr 1832, Elizabeth Still, James Wood, adminrs.

DANIEL KREMER, Montgomery, 20 Apr 1832, John Kremer, Jacob Kremer, adminrs.

DAVID CLEMENS, Gwynedd, 30 Apr 1832, Daniel L. Reiff, John Evans, adminrs.

GEORGE WEBSTER, Moreland, 19 Apr 1832, Charles Webster, adminr.

HENRY HALLMAN, Skippack & Perkiomen, 21 Apr 1832, Jacob Hallman, George Shoemaker, adminrs.

ANDREW GRABER, Upper Hanover, 30 Apr 1832, George Graber, Andrew Graber, adminrs.

JOHN WILLRAHAM, Limerick, 10 May 1832, Elizabeth Willraham, adminr.

JOHN ROBELBERGER, Marlborough, 18 May 1832, Abraham Robelberger, adminr.

ANN WILLS, Plymouth, 22 May 1832, Alan Wills, adminr.

BLUSSANA SLEMER, Franconia, 8 Jun 1832, Daniel Selmer, adminr.

CATHARINE BEAN, Worcester, 11 Jun 1832, Jacob Bean, adminr.

EDWARD BUNK, Upper Dublin, 11 Jun 1832, William Bunk, Isaac Bunk, adminrs.

STEPHEN PORTER, Norriton, 13 Jun 1832, William Hamill, Robert Stinson, adminrs.

GEORGE BOYER, Limerick, 6 Jul 1832, George Boyer, Philip Boyer, John Boyer, Peter Longacker, adminrs.

JOHN RUTHERFORD, Moreland, 21 Jul 1832, Jacob Rutherford, adminr.

JOHN HURPLE, Upper Providence, 30 Jul 1832, Jacob Custer, adminr.

JOHN BEYER, Norriton, 30 Aug 1832, Jacob Beyer, Harry Frick, adminrs.

ABRAHAM WAMBOLD, Franconia, 30 Aug 1832, Abraham Wambold, Samuel Wambold, adminrs.

NATHANIEL M. LEARNARD, Upper Merion, 16 Aug 1832, William Davis, John Supplee, adminrs.

ANN STERNER, Frederick, 20 Aug 1832, John H. Sterner, adminr.

SARAH DRAKE, Montgomery, 20 Aug 1832, Evan Jones, Jacob Fitzwater, adminr.

DERICK HOGELAND, Moreland, 13 Nov 1832, Jane Hogeland, George H. Pawling, adminr.

NICHOLAS MARTIN, Worcester, 13 Nov 1832, Abraham Martin, Cornelius Tyson, adminrs.

THOMAS BROADES, Lower Merion, 16 Nov 1832, Jacob Colflesh, William Colp, adminrs.

JACOB BEARD, Norriton, 19 Nov 1832, David Beard, adminr.

GEORGE WHITE, Plymouth 19 Nov 1832, Jacob White, adminr.

RICHARD BROADES, Lower Merion, 29 Nov 1832, Mary Broades, George Pechin, adminr.

JOHN NICHOLAS MILLER, Upper Hanover, 29 Nov 1832, John Miller, Solomon Fry, adminrs.

DAVID ZELL, Norriton, 4 Dec 1832, Thomas Read, adminr.

JOSEPH REIFSNYDER, New Hanover, 14 Dec 1832, Louis Bickle, adminr.

JESSE COMLY, Moreland, 15 Dec 1832, Jesse Comly, William B. Comly, adminrs.

THOMAS HOLMS, Upper Merion, 21 Dec 1832, Isaac Jones, Jr., adminr.

DANIEL DETWILER, Perkiomen, 22 Dec 1832, Catharine Detwiler, George Reiff, adminrs.

PHILIP SELLERS, Whitemarsh, 24 Dec 1832, Hannah Sellers, adminr.

JOHN LONGAKER, Upper Providence, 24 Dec 1832, John Longaker, Isaac Longaker, adminrs.

MATTHIAS ANDEY, Potts Grove, 26 Dec 1832, David Andey, Henry Andey, adminrs.

ISAAC HALLOWELL, Abington, 26 Dec 1832, Yarnall Hallowell, William Grant, adminrs.

GODFREY DHILE, Lower Merion, 29 Dec 1832, Barbara Dhile, Anthony L. Anderson, adminrs.

SAMUEL BUSH, Whitpain, 29 Dec 1832, James Bush, adminr.

SAMUEL FETTER, Whitpain, 29 Dec 1832, Matthias Fetter, adminr.

EDWARD SPENCER, Horsham, 4 Jan 1833, Cadwallader Spencer, John Kenderdine, adminrs.

ABRAHAM DETWILER, Franconia, 5 Jan 1833, Mary Detwiler, Christian Detwiler, John Hunsicker, adminrs.

ANDREW CASSELBERRY, Lower Providence, 10 Jan 1833, Derrick Casselberry, Arnold Casselberry, adminrs.

JOSEPH MCCLELLAND, Whitemarsh, 15 Jan 1833, Solomon Artman, adminr.

JOHN DAVIS, Worcester, 15 Jan 1833, David Thomas, John Newberry, Baltzer Hoffman, adminrs.

BENJAMIN ROSENBERGER, Hatfield, 21 Jan 1833, Benjamin Rosenberger, Martin Hocker, adminrs.

JESSE SHRIVER, Abington, 21 Jan 1833, Andrew Stewart, adminr.

GEORGE SHIVER, Abington, 21 Jan 1833, Andrew Stewart, adminr.

JOHN MILLER, Upper Providence, 20 Jan 1833, Henry Miller, adminr.

MARTHA TYSON, Upper Dublin, 22 Jan 1833, Peter Tyson, adminr.

SARAH NUNGESSER, Lower Providence, 22 Jan 1833, Samuel Petters, adminr.

SARAH HEEBNER, Norriton, 25 Jan 1833, Joseph Heebner, Isaac Cassel, adminrs.

PHILIP WOLMER, Lower Providence, 14 Feb 1833, Jacob Teany, Jacob Highley, adminrs.

JACOB HENDRICKS, Limerick, 21 Feb 1833, Samuel Hendricks, adminr.

JOHN WILSON, Franconia, 22 Feb 1833, William Wilson, Elina Wilson, adminrs.

JOHN BARNES, Horsham, 28 Mar 1833, Rebecca Barnes, Jonathan Iredell, Jr., adminrs.

JONATHAN CLEAVER, Upper Merion, 22 Feb 1833, Edward Liters, Matthew Roberts, adminrs.

ABRAHAM SOLOMON, Upper Providence, 26 Feb 1833, Henry Fry, adminr.

PHILIP LIDNER, Upper Merion, 9 Mar 1833, William Holstein, adminr.

JACOB DENGLER, Potts Grove, 11 Mar 1833, Sarah Dengler, Henry Dengler, David Gresh, adminrs.

AMOS ELLIS, Norriton, 1 Apr 1833, Catharine Ellis, Isaac Shoemaker, John Styer, adminrs.

ANN MCDERMONT, Norristown, 2 Apr 1833, Isaac Miller, adminr.

ELIZABETH LONG, Upper Merion, 8 Apr 1833, Joseph Crawford, William Crawford, adminrs.

HENRY GRUB, Upper Dublin, 9 Apr 1833, William Burk, adminr.

HENRY HUDDLESON, Norriton, 9 Apr 1833, Isaac Huddleson, John McKay, Mary Huddleston, adminrs.

REV. JOHN T. FABER, New Hanover, 10 Apr 1833, Charles J. Faber, George Hillegass, adminrs.

JOHN RIDER, Upper Merion, 12 Apr 1833, William Hallaway, adminr.

WILLIAM FOULKE, Gwynedd, 13 Apr 1833, William Foulke, Aaron Lukens, adminrs.

JOHN HERIEY, Towamencin, 19 Apr 1833, Jacob Prise, Garrett Metz, adminrs.

PETER DAGER, Whitemarsh, 20 Apr 1833, Elizabeth Dager, William Dewees, adminrs.

JOHN WIREMAN, Limerick, 22 Apr 1833, Samuel Pennypacker, adminr.

SUSANNAH SUPPLEE, 23 Apr 1833, Samuel Supplee, adminr.

JONAS ROYER, Douglass, 24 Apr 1833, Margaret Royer, adminr.

SAMUEL DRESHER, Upper Dublin, 25 Apr 1833, Oliver Dresher, Levi Dresher, adminrs.

JACOB DRESHER, Towamencin, 4 May 1833, Jacob Andrew, Joel Wiegner, adminrs.

CHRISTIAN HERNER, Upper Dublin, 6 May 1833, Jacob Sandman, adminr.

THOMAS FLETCHER, Abington, 10 May 1833, Daniel Fletcher, David Thomas, adminrs.

JESSE KEESEY, Norristown, 11 May 1833, John Keesey, adminr.

JOHN PROTZMAN, Lower Providence, 14 May 1833, Peter Keyser, adminr.

CONRAD PROTZMAN, Lower Providence, 14 May 1833, Peter Keyser, adminr.

JOHN BICKLE, New Hanover, 17 May 1833, John Yerger, adminr.

GEORGE ROBERTS, Gwynedd, 25 May 1833, David Thomas, Evan Jones, adminrs.

JOSEPH FISHER, Norristown, 7 Jun 1833, David Rogers, George M. Potts, adminrs.

REES HARRY, Lower Merion, 1 Jul 1833, John Harry, Edwin Harry, adminrs.

JOSEPH HOLDEMAN, Gwynedd, 22 Jul 1833, Jacob Pruner, Jr., adminr.

GEORGE MCCLENACHAN, Lower Merion, 5 Aug 1833, Mary McCleanachan, adminr.

HENRY STERNMETZ, Pottstown, 19 Aug 1833, Daniel Sternmetz, adminr.

SARAH THOMAS, Whitpain, 19 Aug 1833, David Thomas, adminr.

HANNAH SPENCER, Moreland, 20 Aug 1833, Samuel E. Spencer, adminr.

BARNABAS DIEMER, Plymouth, 2 Sep 1833, John McCann, adminr.

JOHN BICKEL, Douglass, 4 Sep 1833, Lewis Bickel, John Bickel, adminr.

DANIEL BICKEL, Douglass, 14 Sep 1833, Elizabeth Bickel, Henry Gable, adminr.

JOHN WALTON, Moreland, 4 Oct 1833, Caroline Walton, Jacob Saurman, adminrs.

ANN FOX, Skippack, 5 Oct 1833, Isaac Prizer, adminr.

MARY HUBBS, Upper Dublin, 14 Oct 1833, Amos L. Lukens, Lewis Jones, adminrs.

SARAH WILSON, Lower Merion, 15 Oct 1833, Dr. James Anderson, adminr.

DANIEL BORNEMAN, Upper Hanover, 17 Oct 1833, Henry Borneman, John Schwenck, adminrs.

JACOB JOHNSON, Gwynedd, 17 Oct 1833, Jacob Lutz, adminr.

JOSEPH KAUMAN, Norristown, 13 Mar 1833, Tryon Kauman, adminr.

HANNAH ELLIS, Norriton, 19 Oct 1833, John Styer, adminr.

JOHN SNELL, Norristown, 23 Oct 1833, Robert Argue, George M. Potts, adminrs.

JOHN DAVIS, Limerick, 26 Oct 1833, Benjamin Davis, Robert Evans, adminrs.

MARY SNYDER, Hatfield, 28 Oct 1833, Christopher Meshter, John Anders.

ANN LUKENS, Horsham, 1 Nov 1833, Jonathan Jarrett, adminr.

JOHN REIFSNYDER, New Hanover, 2 Nov 1833, Jacob Reifsnyder, Samuel Yerger, adminrs.

GEORGE D. RICHARDS, Douglass, 2 Nov 1833, Adam Whartman, adminr.

JACOB BAUMAN, Douglass, 18 Nov 1833, John Bauman, Isaac Bauman, adminrs.

JOHN C. DETWILER, Lower Providence, 19 Nov 1833, Christian Detwiler, adminr.

BARNEY BURNS, Plymouth, 26 Nov 1833, Hugh Burns, adminr.

THOMAS MARGERUM, Moreland, 3 Dec 1833, Rachel Margerum, adminr.

LEWIS JENKINS, Upper Merion, 6 Dec 1833, James Berry, Phinebas Phillips, adminrs.

JOSEPH SCHRAUGER, Upper Providence, 14 Dec 1833, Abel Fitzwater, adminr.

GEORGE HILLEGASS, Upper Hanover, 19 Dec 1833, Jacob Hillegass, adminr.

JOHN EHLE, Upper Hanover, 23 Dec 1833, Elizabeth Ehle, Conrad Brey, adminrs.

THOMAS JONES, Cheltenham, 27 Dec 1833, Ezra Jones, Joseph Jones, adminrs.

JOHN MOYER, Sr., Franconia, 10 Jan 1834, Jacob Moyer, Jonas Moyer, Isaac Moyer, adminrs.

RICHARD ROBERTS, Cheltenham, 11 Jan 1834, George S. Roberts, adminr.

HENRY ROSENBERGER, Worcester, 21 Jan 1834, John H. Rosenberger, adminr.

HENRY HOFFMAN, Douglass, 21 Jan 1834, George Hoffman, Andrew Hoffman, adminrs.

CHRISTIANA LENHART, Cheltenham, 30 Jan 1834, Joseph Lenhart, adminr.

JOHN DAVIS, Upper Providence, 1 Feb 1834, Abraham Brown, adminr.

JOHN FAST, Springfield, 3 Feb 1834, John Roberts, adminr.

JOHN BENKIS, Upper Hanover, 6 Feb 1834, Andrew Schwartz, adminr.

PHILIP ROSENBERRY, Lower Providence, 11 Feb 1834, Mary Rosenberry, Samuel Rosenberry, adminrs.

EVE HERSTINE, Limerick, 14 Feb 1834, David Herstine, adminr.

JACOB JOHNSON, Springfield, 17 Feb 1834, Elizabeth Johnson, adminr.

RACHEL SUPPLEE, Norriton, 18 Feb 1834, Enoch Supplee, adminr.

PETER SCHWEISFORD, Sr., New Hanover, 18 Feb 1834, John Schweisford, Peter Schweisford, adminrs.

JONAS RAMBO, Worcester, 20 Feb 1834, Margaret Rambo, Robert Argue, adminrs.

PHEBE BARLOW, Limerick, 25 Feb 1834, John Barlow, adminr.

JOSIAH DENNIS, Upper Hanover, 7 Mar 1834, Wilson Dennis, adminr.

CATHARINE YELLIS, Towamencin, 10 Mar 1834, Jacob Hunsberger, George Heugey, adminrs.

ANN RITTENHOUSE, Upper Providence, 20 Mar 1834, Henry R. Rittenhouse, adminr.

SAMUEL YOHN, Potts Grove, 18 Mar 1834, Sarah Yohn, adminr.

JONATHAN SHAY, Horsham, 19 Mar 1834, Margaret Shay, James Paul, adminr.

MARIA UMSTEAD, Lower Providence, 19 Mar 1834, John Umstead, adminr.

MARGARET ENGLE, Douglass, 24 Mar 1834, John Engle, adminr.

MARY CHAIN, 27 Mar 1834, John McFarland, adminr.

PATRICK TOWAL, Whitemarsh, 29 Mar 1834, Dennis O'Brien, adminr.

ABRAHAM GROBB, Potts Grove, 4 Apr 1834, George Grobb, Samuel Grobb, George Mauck, adminrs.

REBECCA EVANS, Limerick, 15 Apr 1834, Robert Evans, adminr.

PHEBE EVANS, Limerick, 15 Apr 1834, David Evans, adminr.

JOHN MEECH, Lower Providence, 21 Apr 1834, Jacob Urich, George Sommerlot, adminrs.

CATHARINE ENGLE, Douglass, 23 Apr 1834, John Engle, adminr.

JACOB SWARTLEY, Sr., Towamencin, 6 May 1834, Catharine Swartley, Jacob Swartley, Jr., adminrs.

JOHN GRIMLEY, New Hanover, 8 May 1834, Henry Smith, Samuel H. Bartolet, adminrs.

CASPER, SNIDER, Lower Providence, 9 May 1834, Daniel Morgan, adminr.

TOBIAS ALLBRIGHT, Frederick, 15 May 1834, Jacob Yost, Daniel Grob, adminrs.

RACHEL SHELMIRE, Moreland, 30 May 1834, John Stevens, adminr.

JACOB WISLER, Hatfield, 7 Jun 1834, Isaac Wisler, adminr.

ISAAC WEBER, Montgomery, 17 Jun 1834, Jacob Weber, adminr.

ROBERT ST. CLAIR, Norriton, 13 Jun 1834, Arthur St. Clair, David Boyd, adminrs.

HENRY R. ALDERFER, Upper Providence, 18 Jul 1834, Margaret Alderfer, Frederick Alderfer, adminrs.

JACOB HEIST, Plymouth, 21 Jul 1834, Thomas Read, adminr.

JACOB LANDIS, Sr., Upper Salford, 29 Jul 1834, Jacob Landis, Jr., Abraham Landis, Jacob Moyer, adminrs.

WILLIAM DORANS, Whitpain, 28 Jul 1834, Robert Kerr, adminr.

DUFFIELD WILLARD, Upper Dublin, 31 Jul 1834, Mary Willard, Griffith Francis, adminrs.

WILLIAM NYCE, Whitpain, 2 Aug 1834, Evan Jones, John Supplee, adminrs.

JOSEPH JOHNSON, Worcester, 6 Aug 1834, Elizabeth Johnson, adminr.

JOSEPH HOUPT, Upper Dublin, 11 Aug 1834, Henry W. Houpt, Christian Keisel, adminrs.

JACOB GARBER, Sr., Limerick, 12 Aug 1834, Benedict Garber, Joshua Croll, adminrs.

ANDREW LONG, Norristown, 12 Aug 1834, George M. Potts, adminr.

MARY H. CONARD, Upper Merion, 12 Aug 1834, Dennis Conard, adminr.

JOHN BEEN, Worcester, 25 Aug 1834, Andrew Been, Jacob Been, adminrs.

PETER SAYLOR, Lower Providence, 2 Sep 1834, Arnold Saylor, John Saylor, adminrs.

ANDREW CRAWFORD, Plymouth, 3 Sep 1834, Alan W. Corson, adminr.

TOBIAS YERGER, New Hanover, 10 Sep 1834, Isaac Yerger, adminr.

REBECCA GRIFFITH, Gwynedd, 15 Sep 1834, Joseph Lowry, Eli Griffith, adminrs.

PHILIP L. MARKLEY, Norristown, 22 Sep 1834, Mary Umstead, adminr.

PETER SAUMAN, Montgomery, 22 Sep 1834, George H. Pawling, adminr.

JOHN DETWEILER, Worcester, 27 Sep 1834, Jacob Detweiler, Henry Detweiler, adminrs.

CATHARINE SWARTZ, Lower Salford, 29 Sep 1834, Andrew Swartz, adminr.

JOHN CASSELBERRY, Lower Providence, 7 Oct 1834, Rebecca Casselberry, William L. Evans, adminrs.

JESSE MILLER, Norristown, 8 Oct 1834, Isaac H. Miller, adminr.

OLIVIA SANDS, Upper Dublin, 9 Oct 1834, Samuel Sands, Joseph Sands, adminrs.

JANE PRICE, Lower Merion, 29 Oct 1834, Samuel Lindsay, Ellis Maris, Jesse Reece, adminrs.

JOHN CLAYTON, Moreland, 3 Nov 1834, Jonathan Clayton, Jacob E. Clayton, Joseph Clayton, adminrs.

MATTHEW DICE, Lower Providence, 6 Nov 1834, John Shearer, adminr.

JOHN WHITE, Plymouth, 7 Nov 1834, John White, adminr.

PHILIP REES, Upper Merion, 14 Nov 1834, Elizabeth Rees, John Rees, Enoch Richards, adminrs.

JOHN HOFFMAN, Marlborough, 17 Nov 1834, Philip Reed, Daniel Freas, adminrs.

PETER STELTZ, New Hanover, 17 Nov 1834, Samuel Steltz, Lewis Steltz, adminrs.

JOHN BISBING, Horsham, 18 Nov 1834, William Earnest, Jacob Pruner, Jr., adminrs.

SAMUEL THOMAS, Sr., Cheltenham, 24 Nov 1834, Harvey Thomas, Samuel Thomas, adminrs.

ABRAHAM HENDRICKS, Towamencin, 27 Nov 1834, Benjamin Hendricks, adminr.

THOMAS FERGUSON, Horsham, 27 Nov 1834, George H. Pawling, adminr.

WILLIAM ROBERTS, Moreland, 27 Nov 1834, John Engart, adminr.

SAMUEL DETWEILER, New Hanover, 22 Dec 1834, Samuel Detweiler, William Shide, adminrs.

CATHARINE WAMPOLE, Towamencin, 27 Dec 1834, Frederick Wampole, adminr.

FRANCIS A. REED, Frederick, 7 Jan 1835, John Reed, adminr.

JOHN FILLMAN, Upper Hanover, 19 Jan 1835, George Billger, adminr.

BENJAMIN WENTZ, Whitpain, 19 Jan 1835, John Heist, William Wentz, adminrs.

JOHN NEWMAN, New Hanover, 19 Jan 1835, Henry Smith, adminr.

ABRAHAM ASHENFELTER, Limerick, 19 Jan 1835, Barbara Ashenfelter, Robert Umstead, adminrs.

ELIZABETH REES, Lower Providence, 19 Jan 1835, William Rees, adminr.

HENRY SCHATZ, Upper Salford, 25 Jan 1835, Jacob Schatz, adminr.

SAMUEL BRANT, Limerick, 31 Jan 1835, Isaac Brant, Michael Brant, Jeremiah Christman, adminrs.

MARY TYSON, Cheltenham, 31 Jan 1835, Jonathan Mather, John L. Williams, adminrs.

HANNAH GARBER, Upper Providence, 11 Feb 1835, Charles Garber, adminr.

AARON RAMBO, Upper Merion, 14 Feb 1835, Benjamin Rambo, adminr.

WILLIAM YERKES, Lower Salford, 16 Feb 1835, Abraham Yerkes, Jacob Kolb, adminrs.

ARTHUR T. MCFARLAND, Norriton, 8 Feb 1835, John Shannon, adminr.

ELIZABETH FREDERICK, Douglass, 3 Mar 1835, John Frederick, adminr.

JOHN KENDIG, Hatfield, 9 Mar 1835, Jacob Kendig, Joseph Kendig, adminrs.

JACOB FOX, Sr., Limerick, 16 Mar 1835, Jacob Fox, Jr., adminr.

CHRISTOPHER HITNER, Whitemarsh, 19 Mar 1835, Christopher Hitner, adminr.

EVE MARIA SCHWENCK, Gwynedd, 24 Mar 1835, William Schwenck, Jacob Schwenck, Peter Summers, adminrs.

ROBERT COULSTON, Norristown, 27 Mar 1835, Timothy C. Boyle, adminr.

BARBARA BENNER, Franconia, 28 Mar 1835, Abraham Benner, Christian Benner, adminrs.

BARBARA JOHNSON, Skippack, 4 Apr 1835, Jacob Johnson, adminr.

CONRAD AMICH, Upper Dublin, 13 Apr 1835, Henry Scheetz, adminr.

JOHN JONES, Whitemarsh, 14 Apr 1835, John Major, adminr.

REES THOMAS, Upper Merion, 16 Apr 1835, Rebecca Thomas, William B. Thomas, adminrs.

SOPHIA ROSENBERGER, Hatfield, 25 Apr 1835, John W. Rosenberger, Jacob Rosenberger, adminrs.

HIRAM BARNES, 2 May 1835, William White, adminr.

ISAAC ZIMMERMAN, Whitpain, 11 May 1835, Jacob Zimmerman, William Zimmerman, adminrs.

SARAH HESS, Lower Providence, 12 May 1835, John Osborn, Jesse Kneezel, adminrs.

BARABRA WAGGONER, Limerick, 15 May 1835, Jacob Foust, adminr.

HANNAH SHOEMAKER, Gwynedd, 18 May 1835, Thomas Shoemaker, adminr.

CATHARINE, ALBEBACK, Hatfield, 23 May 1835, Abraham Albeback, adminr.

ELIZABETH STAGNER, Montgomery, 28 May 1835, Henry Stagner, adminr.

REBECCA WILLS, Potts Grove, 29 May 1835, William Wills, adminr.

GEORGE BISBING, Sr., Whitemarsh, 10 Jun 1835, Catharine Bisbing, George Bisbing, Jr., Joseph Kirkner, William Bisbing, adminrs.

HENRY MCCOLLOM, Norristown, 23 Jun 1835, Samuel Sherwood, adminr.

HANNAH MARPLE, Plymouth, 27 Jun 1835, William Wills, adminr.

DANIEL BEARD, Upper Providence, 6 Jul 1835, David Beard, adminr.

JOHN BEARD, Lower Providence, 6 Jul 1835, David Beard, adminr.

JOSEPH BEARD, 6 Jul 1835, David Beard, adminr.

LYDIA SHAMBO, Lower Providence, 20 Jul 1835, John Getty, Philip Shambo, adminrs.

MICHAEL BUTTERWEEK, Upper Hanover, 21 July 1835, Joseph Butt, adminr.

JACOBINA GERKIS, Lower Salford, 1 Aug 1835, Abraham Gerkis, adminr.

ELIZABETH DAVES, Plymouth, 3 Aug 1835, William Keiger, Daniel Smith, adminrs.

GEORGE KEIGER, Plymouth, 3 Aug 1835, William Keiger, Daniel Smith, adminrs.

GEORGE SCHNEIDER, Montgomery, 10 Aug 1835, Christian Schneider, Samuel Vanhorn, adminrs.

HENRY FREDERICK, Douglass, 17 Aug 1835, John Frederick, Jonas Fox, adminrs.

MARY RITTENHOUSE, Skippack, 29 Aug 1835, David Derstine, adminr.

LUCETTA WELLS, Norristown, 4 Sep 1835, Thomas Wells, adminr.

SAMUEL ADAMS, Upper Merion, 11 Sep 1835, John B. Adams, adminr.

JOHN BLYLER, Douglass, 29 Sep 1835, John Blyler, William Johnson, adminrs.

HENRY BOYER, New Hanover, 29 Sep 1835, Andrew Hoffman, Henry Knetz, adminrs.

ISRAEL YOCUM, Hatfield, 9 Oct 1835, Sarah Yocum, Enos Lukens, adminrs.

JACOB FRY, Lower Providence, 14 Oct 1835, Peter Warner, Samuel Huser, adminrs.

ANTHONY MILLER, Hatfield, 20 Oct 1835, Benjamin Miller, adminr.

EZRA JONES, Cheltenham, 23 Oct 1835, Joel Woolman, Solomon Jones, adminrs.

HENRY ZEIBER, Marlborough, 6 Nov 1835, Jacob Long, adminr.

PHILIP GABLE, Sr., Upper Salford, 6 Nov 1835, Charles Gable, Philip Gable, adminrs.

GOTTSHALK GOTTSHALK, Towamencin, 16 Nov 1835, Garrett Gottshalk, Henry Gottshalk, adminrs.

HENRY TRUMBAUER, Limerick, 20 Nov 1835, John Trumbauer, Abraham, Hallman, adminr.

SUSANNA ROSENBERRY, Skippack, 26 Nov 1835, Jacob J. Hunsicker, adminr.

GARDENER LATCH, Lower Merion, 4 Dec 1835, Henrietta Latch, Francis H. Latch, adminrs.

SALOMEY SPECHT, Potts Grove, 4 Dec 1835, George Zealer, adminr.

MARY MORGAN, Hatfield, 5 Dec 1835, Mary Ann Morgan, adminr.

DAVID WEAVEL, Gwynedd, 12 Dec 1835, Mary Neavel, Wyant Neavel, adminrs.

PATRICK HOGAN, Lower Merion, 14 Dec 1835, Thomas Crowley, adminr.

ENOS JACOBY, Norristown, 24 Dec 1835, John Zeiber, Charles Jones, adminrs.

CHRISTIAN GOTTWALS, Upper Providence, 30 Dec 1835, John Baser, John Rosenberry, adminrs.

DANIEL RAMBO, Upper Merion, 9 Jan 1836, Jonathan Cleaver Rambo, adminr.

JOHN WALD, Limerick, 27 Jan 1836, John Winter, Jr., adminr.

WILLIAM SAMPLY, Towamencin, 6 Feb 1836, Barbara Samply, Jesse Samply, adminrs.

JOHN BRAND, Moreland, 16 Feb 1836, Jonathan Lukens, adminr.

JOHN PRIZER, Sr., Upper Providence, 6 Feb 1836, Abraham Hallman, adminr.

WILLIAM BURNEY, Montgomery, 23 Feb 1836, Hannah Burney, Benjamin Evans, adminrs.

JAMES YOCUM, Sr., Franconia, 25 Feb 1836, Benjamin Yocum, James Yocum, adminrs.

SOPHIA RHOADES, Moreland, 26 Feb 1836, George H. Pawling, adminr.

JACOB WILLFONG, Lower Merion, 3 Mar 1836, John Dauley, adminr.

CHARLES OTTINGER, Springfield, 4 Mar 1836, Mary Ottinger, John Huston, adminrs.

DANIEL SCHWENK, Frederick, 11 Mar 1836, Daniel Schwenk, Henry Daub, Abraham Stetler, John Christian, adminrs.

JOHN RICHARD, 14 Mar 1836, Robert H. Richard, Henry Hoffman, adminrs.

DENNIS O'BRIEN, 19 Mar 1836, Samuel Garber, adminr.

SAMUEL BURK, 20 Mar 1836, Edward Burk, adminr.

JAMES SHOEMAKER, 28 Mar 1836, Spencer Shoemaker, adminr.

YELLIS CASSEL, Hatfield, 29 Mar 1836, Harry Overholtzer, John Drake, adminrs.

MARTHA MCCARTER, Upper Merion, 1 Mar 1836, Eli McCarter, adminr.

MARGARET HUNSICKER, Worcester, 4 Apr 1836, Michael Zilling, Henry Lederack, Jr., adminrs.

GEORGE FIE, Whitemarsh, 9 Apr 1836, John Hiltner, Andrew Fie, adminrs.

THOMAS MCGLENON, Lower Merion, 15 Apr 1836, Thomas McGlenon, adminr.

ANN SMITH, Marlborough, 28 Apr 1836, John Haring, adminr.

JOHN ENGLE, Sr., Douglass, 7 May 1836, Susannah Engle, John Engle, Jr., adminrs.

ABRAHAM GEYER, Douglass, 7 May 1836, Sophia Geyer, Gabriel Schweinhart, adminrs.

BARBARA ROSENBERGER, Hatfield, 18 May 1836, John Rosenberger, adminr.

MARTHA B. HICKS, Montgomery, 21 May 1836, Alfred Thomas, adminr.

PETER HEISLER, Gwynedd, 21 May 1836, Catharine Heisler, Henry Kneedler, adminrs.

BENJAMIN WOLF, Whitemarsh, 18 Jul 1836, Catharine Wolf, George M. Potts, William Thomas, George Dager, adminrs.

GEORGE A. SHELL, Moreland, 18 Jul 1836, George Fetter, Jacob Shelmire, Amos Addie, adminrs.

ANTHONY KEHL, Douglass, 25 Jul 1836, Moses Kehl, Anthony Kehl, George Kehl, adminrs.

SARAH EGBERT, Lower Providence, 25 Jul 1836, Thomas Egbert, adminr.

JACOB STILWAGON, 18 Aug 1836, Philip Stong, adminr.

MARY RASSE, Hatfield, 30 Jul 1836, Philip Rasse, adminr.

MARY EVANS, Limerick, 16 Aug 1836, Robert Evans, adminr.

MARY WALNUT, Montgomery, 22 Aug 1836, Jerome Walnut, adminr.

ANDREW HORN, Lower Merion, 25 Aug 1836, Henry Beavan, adminr.

MARY KERBAUGH, Upper Dublin, 14 Sep 1836, Isaac Strunk, adminr.

WILLIAM RHOADS, Norristown, 15 Sep 1836, John H. Slingloff, Cornelius Rhoads, adminrs.

EDWARD SHARP, Upper Merion, 24 Sep 1836, David R. Kennedy, adminr.

GEORGE COOK, Upper Merion, 28 Sep 1836, Jane Cook adminr.

PETER RAMBO, 3 Oct 1836, J. Cleaver Rambo, Irvins Rambo, adminrs.

NORMAN CLAYTON, 13 Oct 1836, Mary Clayton, adminr.

JACOB MILLER, 15 Oct 1836, William Miller, adminr.

MICHAEL WEYERMAN, 18 Oct 1836, Michael Weyerman, John Bergey, adminrs.

RACHEL HOGE, 20 Oct 1836, Abraham Benner, adminr.

NATHAN LUKENS, 22 Oct 1836, Samuel Shoemaker, Asa Comley, adminrs.

CATHARINE ROSENBERGER, 26 Oct 1836, Abraham Rosenberger, adminr.

PETER CLEVER, Cheltenham, 2 Nov 1836, John Clever, William Bradfield, adminrs.

SUSANNA HEEBNER, 4 Nov 1836, John Hoffman, adminr.

WILLIAM MOORE, Lower Providence, 4 Nov 1836, Christian Detwiler, adminr.

HENRY GARLY, Upper Dublin, 5 Nov 1836, John M. Jones, adminr.

JOHN HICKEY, Norriton, 7 Nov 1736, George M. Potts, adminr.

MARY HARLEY, Towamencin, 11 Nov 1836, Margaret Harley, Jacob Metz, adminrs.

JOSEPH YEAKLE, 21 Nov 1836, Jacob Pruner, Jr., adminr.

PHILIP LAVER, Montgomery, 24 Nov 1836, John Evans, adminr.

DAVID MOORE, Lower Providence, 28 Nov 1836, Christian Detwiler, adminr.

JOSEPH SMITH, Lower Merion, 30 Nov 1836, Catharine W. Smith, adminr.

GILBERT W. HICKS, Moreland, 6 Dec 1836, James M. Hicks, Lemen Barnes, adminrs.

HENRY COLE, Worcester, 9 Dec 1836, Abraham C. Cole, adminr.

JACOB RICHARDS, Pottstown, 10 Dec 1836, George Richards, adminr.

SAMUEL ATKINSON, Upper Merion, 20 Dec 1836, John Atkinson, adminr.

JOHN BAKER, Lower Providence, 12 Dec 1836, Silas Baker, adminr.

LEONARD VANFOSSEN, Norriton, 15 Dec 1836, Matthias Brumback, adminr.

JOHN CLYMER, Lower Salford, 5 Jan 1836, Jacob Clymer, Daniel Boorse, adminrs.

THOMAS WAKEFIELD, Moreland, 6 Jan 1837, Joseph B. Yerkes, adminr.

ABRAHAM CUSTER, Perkiomen & Skippack, 23 Jan 1837, Peter Custer, David Gottshall, adminrs.

JACOB HARTZELL, Upper Salford, 27 Jan 1837, John Hartzell, David Hartzell, adminrs.

MARGARET CROMWELL, Upper Providence, 30 Jan 1837, Joseph Hunsicker, adminr.

JACOB BEALER, Lower Merion, 4 Feb 1837, Mary Bealer, adminr.

JESSE HOLT, Plymouth, 7 Feb 1837, William Webster, Warner Holt, adminrs.

JOHN HENDRICKS, Towamencin, 10 Feb 1837, Abraham Delp, Jacob Kulp, Jr., adminrs.

JACOB BEAVER, Limerick, 11 Feb 1837, Barnhard Keeler, adminr.

JOHN MARTERSON, Plymouth, 14 Feb 1837, George Martin, John Hocker, adminr.

REBECCA KIRK, Upper Dublin, 20 Feb 1837, John L. Kirk, Jane Kirk, adminrs.

JOHN ROBERTS, Montgomery, 20 Feb 1837, Samuel Cadwallader, adminr.

CATHARINE SCHWENK, Frederick, 20 Feb 1837, Daniel Boyer, adminr.

JOHN ROBERTS, Lower Merion, 22 Feb 1837, William W. Roberts, Isaac W. Roberts, adminrs.

REESE PRICE, Lower Merion, 22 Feb 1837, Ellis Maris, adminr.

JOSEPH FULTON, Upper Providence, 22 Feb 1837, Martha Fulton, Daniel Morgan, adminrs.

CHRISTIAN STEANRUCK, Potts Grove, 23 Feb 1837, Isaac Steanruck, adminr.

DAVID DAVIS, Plymouth, 25 Feb 1837, Thomas Read, adminr.

CHARLOTTE DAVIS, Plymouth, 25 Feb 1837, Thomas Read, adminr.

JACOB SPECE, Limerick, 2 Mar 1837, John Spece, adminr.

SARAH STEVENS, Upper Merion, 7 Mar 1837, James B. Stevens, adminr.

JOHN WYNKOOPE, Moreland, 10 Mar 1837, Amos Addis, adminr.

JOHN S. BRUCKNUM, 22 Mar 1837, George M. Potts, adminr.

MARY LENTZ, Lower Merion, 27 Mar 1837, Benjamin Lentz, adminr.

CHRISTIAN BARDO, Potts Grove, 30 Mar 1837, Daniel Gilbert, George Bickle, adminrs.

CATHARINE HALLMAN, Gwynedd, 1 Apr 1837, Henry Hallman, Jacob Dannehower, adminrs.

PETER HOFFMAN, Gwynedd, 8 Apr 1837, Samuel D. Hoffman, adminr.

CATHARINE MCCROSSON, Worcester, 7 Apr 1837, John Weber, adminr.

JOHN BECHTEL, Upper Hanover, 10 Apr 1837, Jacob Bechtel, John Bechtel, adminrs.

MARY HICK, Norristown, 13 Apr 1837, Susan Green, adminr.

JACOB FILLMAN, Upper Salford, 17 Apr 1837, John Deetz, John Nese, adminrs.

CATHARINE SANDS, Lower Providence, 22 Apr 1837, John Sands, adminr.

JOHN W. ROSENBERGER, Hatfield, 9 Apr 1837, John Frick, Jr., adminr.

FREDERICK RATZEL, Hatfield, 5 May 1837, Jacob Ratzel, Enos Ratzel, adminrs.

BARBARA KULP, Towamencin, 6 May 1837, Jacob Kulp, Jr., John Kulp, Henry Swartley, adminrs.

JONAS SPARE, Upper Providence, 8 May 1837, John E. Spare, adminr.

DAVID WILSON, Whitemarsh, 8 May 1837, Edith Wilson, William Jeans, adminrs.

HENRY B. MESSIMER, Potts Grove, 22 May 1837, John S. Messimer, Joseph Messimer adminrs.

SUSANNA PAUL, Skippack & Perkiomen, 30 May 1837, Samuel Paul, Christian Miller, George Buckwalter, adminrs.

WILLIAM ELLIS, Whitpain, 30 May 1937, Isaac Ellis, Jonathan Ellis, James Hall, adminrs.

MARY HOBSON, Batavia, NY, 10 Jun 1837, John Hobson, adminr.

BERNHARD DOTTS, Whitpain, 1 Jul 1837, John Shenberger, Henry Dotts, adminrs.

DEITER GEIGER, Limerick, 31 Jul 1837, Jacob Geiger, Daniel Geiger, John Brook, adminrs.

RICHARD SHOEMAKER, Horsham, 5 Aug 1837, Job Roberts, Evan Jones, adminrs.

WILLIAM DEROUGH, Lower Providence, 5 Aug 1837, Elizabeth Derough, Moses Bear, adminrs.

JOSEPH ACUFF, Whitpain, 20 Aug 1837, John Sheneberger, adminr.

ELI CARVER, Horsham, 22 Aug 1837, Christian Keisel, adminr.

CHRISTIAN SANDMAN, Moreland, 22 Aug 1837, James Paul, Isaac Walton, adminrs.

HENRY CUSTER, Worcester, 2 Sep 1837, Mathias Brumback, Isaac Johnson, adminrs.

ARNOLD ZIMMERMAN, Worcester, 2 Sep 1837, Mathias Brumback, Isaac Johnson, adminrs.

MARY STAUFFER, Pottstown, 9 Sep 1837, George D. Keim, John M. Keim, adminrs.

JOHN BURGER, Upper Hanover, 11 Sep 1837, Michael Grey, David Grey, adminrs.

JACOB BICKLEY, Whitemarsh, 11 Sep 1837, Hannah Bickley, John R. Umstead, adminrs.

JACOB JOHNSON, Worcester, 19 Sep 1837, Benjamin Johnson, John Reese, adminrs.

BENJAMIN HAGY, Upper Dublin, 22 Sep 1837, John Hagy, adminr.

GEORGE MOYER, Marlborough, 25 Sep 1837, Isaac Moyer, John Moyer, adminrs.

LEAH CRAWFORD, Montgomery, 25 Sep 1837, John Shearer, adminr.

JACOB ZOLLER, New Hanover, 28 Sep 1837, George Zoller, John Gilbert, adminrs.

EDWARD SHARP, Upper Merion, 5 Oct 1837, Robert Sharp, adminr.

JOSEPH MCVAUGH, Montgomery, 6 Oct 1837, John Gordon, adminr.

NICHOLAS FOUST, Frederick, 7 Oct 1837, Peter Foust, Jacob Foust, adminrs.

YEAMANS PAUL, Horsham, 9 Oct 1837, Lukens Paul, Joseph Paul, John Iredell, Jr., adminrs.

PETER LIVERGUTH, Potts Grove, 17 Oct 1837, Daniel Liverguth, Jacob Liverguth, adminrs.

JACOB FRITZ, Potts Grove, 19 Oct 1837, Mary Fritz, Levi Fritz, adminrs.

DANIEL MILLER, Limerick, 24 Oct 1837, John Miller, adminr.

ABRAHAM SHIPE, Hatfield, 30 Oct 1837, Henry Shipe, Yellis Cassel, adminrs.

BENJAMIN DAVIS, Lower Providence, 3 Nov 1837, Nathan Davis, Jesse Davis, adminrs.

PHILIP HURST, Sr., Gwynedd, 4 Nov 1837, Daniel Thomas, Christian Keisel, adminrs.

LAWRENCE SANDMAN, Moreland, 6 Nov 1837, Jacob Sandman, adminr.

JOB DAVIS, Upper Providence, 13 Nov 1837, Elizabeth Davis, James Davis, Joseph Halloway, adminrs.

JACOB MILLER, Upper Hanover, 15 Nov 1837, Daniel Miller, Peter Miller, adminrs.

JACOB HAUCH, Frederick, 20 Nov 1837, Charles Hauch, Simon Hauch, adminrs.

CATHARINE HENDRICKS, Towamencin, 20 Nov 1837, Abraham Delp, Jacob Culp, adminrs.

CHRISTOPHER OTTINGER, Cheltenham, 20 Nov 1837, Ann Ottinger, Charles Heist, adminrs.

ISAAC VANCLEAVE, Moreland, 22, Nov 1837, Benjamin Vancleave, adminr.

MICHAEL WHELAN, Upper Merion, 23 Nov 1837, Miles Kahon, adminr.

WILLIAM E. DAVIS, Gwynedd, 23 Nov 1837, Evan Jones, Lewis Jones, adminrs.

MARTIN HUNSBERGER, Hatfield, 28 Nov 1837, Martin Hunsberger, Joseph Hunsberger, adminrs.

JOHN JONES, Princeton, NJ, 29 Nov 1837, John Lowry, Emley Oden, adminr.

FELIX FRANCIS, Lower Providence, 7 Dec 1837, George Highly, Jacob Kulp, Henry Lonks, Thomas Sheppard, adminrs.

THOMAS CONLEY, Whitemarsh, 22 Dec 1837, Michael Bradley, Catharine Bradley, adminrs.

JEREMIAH BERREL, Abington, 23 Dec 1837, Jeremiah Berrel, adminr.

MARGARET HALLOWELL, Norriton, 26 Dec 1837, Samuel Pluck, adminr.

HENRY BEAVER, Gwynedd, 27 Dec 1837, Barbara Beaver, Frederick Beaver, adminrs.

MERCHANT DAVIS, Plymouth, 2 Jan 1838, Marple Davis, adminr.

ELIZABETH SHENDAM, Norristown, 3 Jan 1838, Henry Frick, adminr.

JACOB HECKLER, Lower Salford, 3 Jan 1838, Fronica Heckler, Joseph Heckler, adminrs.

JACOB FISHER, Frederick, 8 Jan 1838, Jacob Fisher, Joseph Fisher, adminrs.

MARY BITTING Upper Hanover, 11 Jan 1838, Anthony S. Heebner, adminr.

CHRISTIAN HACKMAN, Hatfield, 13 Jan 1838, John Rosenberger, adminr.

WILLIAM P. PRICE, Lower Merion, 22 Jan 1838, Paul Jones, Silas Jones, adminrs.

THOMAS SAULVAMY, Whitemarsh, 24 Jan 1838, Thomas Read, adminr.

RACHEL FREAS, Whitemarsh, 27 Jan 1838, John Freas, adminr.

JOHN STETLER, Potts Grove, 10 Feb 1838, Matthias Geist, Henry Geist, adminrs.

CHARLES WARNER, Gwynedd, 14 Feb 1838, Jacob Fisher, John Kuhler, adminrs.

JOHN MEREDITH, Plymouth, 19 Feb 1838, Jesse Meredith, Moses Lukens, adminrs.

JACOB ZINK, Frederick, 19 Feb 1838, Jacob Zink, adminr.

HANNAH SHAFFER, Limerick, 20 Feb 1838, Peter Shaffer, adminr.

RACHEL JARRET, Horsham, 20 Feb 1838, Jacob E. Jarret, Charles Jarret, adminrs.

ABRAHAM STOVER, Towamencin, 27 Feb 1838, Catharine Stover, Matthias Stover, adminrs.

JOHN CRUNVACK, Sr., Montgomery, 28 Feb 1838, George L. Mosely, adminr.

JOHN HILL, New Hanover, 1 Mar 1838, Daniel Boyer, adminr.

ABRAHAM CLEMMER, Franconia, 7 Mar 1838, Abraham Clemmer, John Clemmer, adminrs.

ROBERT STEWART, Upper Merion, 20 Mar 1838, Samuel H. Coates, adminr.

HENRY PATTZGROFF, New Hanover, 27 Mar 1838, Frederick Dallicker, Thomas Moll, adminrs.

HANNAH SNYDER, Frederick, 29 Mar 1838, Jacob Snyder, adminr.

TACY STYER, Whitpain, 29 Mar 1838, Jacob Styer, Stephen Styer, Charles Styer, adminrs.

BARBARA VANDERFLEET, Norristown, 9 Apr 1838, James Shaw, adminr.

SAMUEL KEELER, New Hanover, 9 Apr 1838, Joseph Keeler, adminr.

MARY STALL, Limerick, 16 Apr 1838, John Dismont, adminr.

JOHN BENNELL, Abington, 16 Apr 1838, Hannah Bennell, Enos Boucher, adminrs.

MATTHEW HARRISON, Upper Merion, 3 May 1838, Andrew Keiger, William Keiger, adminrs.

WILLIAM CUTH, Abington, 8 May 1838, Andrew Manno, adminr.

WILLIAM SHIPS, Moreland, 11 May 1838, Daniel Ships, adminr.

DAVID KLINE, Towamencin, 12 May 1838, Rachel Kline, George Kline, adminrs.

MARGARET BORNE, Lower Salford, 23 May 1838, John Borne, Peter Borne, adminrs.

AZOR LUKENS, Upper Dublin, 26 May 1838, Charles J. Lukens, adminr.

HENRY MILLER, Potts Grove, 31 May 1838, Jacob Mauge, adminr.

BALTZER EARNEST, Upper Dublin, 1 Jun 1838, William Earnest, adminr.

NANCY HEEBNER, 13 Jun 1838, George Heebner, adminr.

ISAAC H. RAMSEY, Upper Merion, 13 Jun 1838, Charles Jones, adminr.

THOMAS T. ROBINSON, Montgomery, 14 Jun 1838, Abigail Robinson, John Evans, adminrs.

JOHN FREIS, Marlborough, 14 Jun 1838, John Freis, Jacob H. Geyer, adminrs.

MACH THOMSON, Abington, 28 Jun 1838, Sarah Thomson, adminr.

CATHARINE DEAN, Whitpain, 28 Jun 1838, Elizabeth Dean, adminr.

JACOB SANDMAN, Gwynedd, 23 Jul 1838, Sarah Sandman, Elizabeth Sandman, John Fitzgerald, adminrs.

MICHAEL SHOEMAKER, Franconia, 24 Jul 1838, Michael Shoemaker, adminr.

JACOB BUCKWALTER, Upper Providence, 25 Jul 1838, Joseph Buckwalter, George Buckwalter, adminrs.

BENJAMIN REES, Gwynedd, 26 Jul 1838, John Rees, Andrew Ambler, adminrs.

MARY EVANS, Limerick, 27 Jul 1838, Robert Evans, adminr.

WILLIAM LUKENS, Norristown, 2 Aug 1838, Amos Lukens, adminr.

GEORGE CONARD, Moreland, 3 Aug 1838, Asa Comly, Thomas Hillburn, adminrs.

OWEN DIGMAN, Upper Merion, 7 Aug 1838, John O'Neil, adminr.

LAWRENCE SANDMAN, Moreland 24 Sep 1838, George H. Pawling, adminr.

LEWIS HANSELL, Lower Merion, 20 Aug 1838, Isaac Hansell, adminr.

SAMUEL MAULSBY, Whitemarsh, 20 Aug 1838, Jonathan Maulsby, Charles Jarrett, adminrs.

BENJAMIN ALDERFER, Lower Salford, 21 Aug 1838, Elizabeth Alderfer, Jacob Alderfer, adminrs.

JAMES SHEETZ, Whitemarsh, 4 Sep 1838, Hannah Sheetz, Henry Sheetz, adminrs.

EMANUEL STITLE, Gwynedd 7 Sep 1838, Samuel Heffenstin, adminr.

THOMAS SHAY, Horsham, 28 Sep 1838, Lewis Jones, adminr.

WILLIAM MULLEN, Moreland, 24 Sep 1838, Joseph Yerkes, adminr.

ABRAHAM HALLMAN, Limerick, 24 Sep 1838, John Hallman, William Hallman, Abraham Hallman, adminrs.

ELIZABETH DETTERER, Worcester, 1 Oct 1838, Christian Detterer, Jacob Detterer, adminrs.

JOHN ADAM DOME, Franconia, 5 Oct 1838, Margaret Dome, Enos Dome, adminrs.

DANIEL SCHWENHART, Potts Grove, 10 Oct 1838, George Schwenhart, Gabriel Schwenhart, adminrs.

ELIZABETH ROSENBERGER, Hatfield, 12 Oct 1838, Isaac Rosenberger, adminr.

MARY KLINE, Norristown, 18 Oct 1838, Isaac Kline, adminr.

DANIEL PAUL, Skippack, 16 Oct 1838, Benjamin Pennebecker, adminr.

FRANCIS T. BOYER, Lower Providence, 18 Oct 1838, Henry Boyer, adminr.

JOHN BAUMAN, New Hanover, 29 Oct 1838, Daniel Pennepacker, adminr.

CHRISTOPHER MATTHIAS, Plymouth, 15 Nov 1838, George M. Potts, adminr.

JACOB SCHAFFER, Marlborough, 19 Nov 1838, Joseph Geiger, adminr.

MARY RUTH, Hatfield, 19 Nov 1838, Jacob Ruth, adminr.

DANIEL BICKEL, Douglass, 19 Nov 1838, Henry Bickel, Daniel Bickel, adminrs.

MARY HALLOWELL, Abington, 20 Nov 1838, Thomas Paul, adminr.

JONATHAN JONES, Worcester, 1 Dec 1838, Robert M. Mingers, Isaac Jones, adminrs.

MICHAEL MOORE, 4 Dec 1838, Mary Moore, Charles Moore, adminrs.

SARAH HOLT, Plymouth, 7 Dec 1838, Warner Holt, adminr.

PHILIP FIE, Whitemarsh, 29 Dec 1838, Andrew Fie, Philip Fie, Jr., adminrs.

HENRY W. HARTZELL, Upper Salford, 3 Jan 1839, Paul Hartzell, Henry Hartzell, adminrs.

PATRICK O'BRIEN, Norristown, 14 Jan 1839, Thomas B. Boileau, adminr.

JOHN MALSBERGER, Potts Grove, 14 Jan 1839, Jacob Manger, adminr.

ABRAHAM HEEBNER, Worcester, 19 Jan 1839, Jacob Heebner, Abraham Heebner, adminrs.

HENRY HARNER, Whitemarsh, 5 Feb 1839, Loyd Jones, adminr.

MARY HALLMAN, Springfield, 19 Feb 1839, Henry Hallman, adminr.

ELIZABETH HUBER, 25 Feb 1839, Jacob H. Huber, adminr.

HANNAH BICKLEY, 26 Feb 1839, John R. Umstead, adminr.

HENRY KOLB, Sr., 20 Mar 1839, Henry Kolb, Isaac Kolb, adminrs.

JACOB BEALER, 26 Mar 1839, Thomas Bealer, adminr.

SAMUEL WEST, 8 Apr 1839, James Paul, adminr.

DANIEL DEAL, 9 Apr 1839, George M. Potts, adminr.

HENRY HILLEGAS, Marlborough, 15 Apr 1839, Jonas Hillegas, David Weidner, adminrs.

ABRAHAM ANDERS, Towamencin, 15 Apr 1839, Christopher Master, adminr.

SAMUEL FRY, Upper Providence, 16 Apr 1839, Jacob Ketler, adminr.

ELIZABETH ROBINSON, 18 Apr 1839, Nathan Robinson, adminr.

LEVI JARRETT, Upper Dublin, 1 May 1839, James White, adminr.

MOSES MCLEAN, 4 May 1839, John McClean, Isaac L. Shoemaker, adminrs.

THOMAS SCARLET, 7 May 1839, Robert Scarlet, Mary Ann Scarlet, adminrs.

WARNER HOLT, 7 May 1839, Rachel S. Holt, Thomas Livezey, adminrs.

SARAH HOLT, 7 May 1839, Seth Holt, adminr.

THOMAS MICHENOR, Moreland, 20 May 1839, Philip Lauer, Jonathan Lukens, adminrs.

THOMAS EGBERT, Whitemarsh, 3 Jun 1839, Margaret Egbert, Samuel Roberts, Isacker R. Egbert, adminrs.

JOHN DAVIS, 8 Jun 1839, Rachel Davis, Francis Dimond, adminrs.

JOSEPH W. THOMAS, 20 Jun 1839, William Thomas, adminr.

GEORGE HORTENSTINE, Lower Providence, 21 Jun 1839, Charles Corson, adminr.

CATHARINE IRCIH, 26 Jun 1839, Michael Pugh, adminr.

MARY ANN BABE, 26 Jun 1839, Michael Pugh, adminr.

JOHN READ, Lower Providence, 28 Jun 1839, William Bean, adminr.

JAMES YOCUM, Norristown, 29 Jun 1839, James Yocum, adminr.

CHRISTIAN FISHER, 1 Jul 1839, Israel Gilbert, adminr.

JOHN S. HALLMAN, Whitpain, 15 Jul 1839, John Hovensack, Wilkin Hovensack, adminrs.

MICHAEL YOUNG, 20 Jul 1839, Elizabeth Young, Isaac Young, adminrs.

ANTHONY BENEZETT, M.D., 13 Aug 1839, Thomas Roberts, adminr.

JOHN KNETZ, 19 Aug 1839, Jonas Knetz, adminr.

SAMUEL GROSS, 20 Aug 1839, John E. Gross, Thomas J. Gross, Jacob Fry, Jr., adminr.

JONAS RAMBO, 5 Sep 1839, John Dismant, Frederick Bergstresser, adminrs.

SARAH MAXWELL, 17 Sep 1839, Thomas Maxwell, adminr.

WILLIAM MULLIA, Horsham, 7 Sep 1839, Amos L. Lukens, adminr.

JESSE ROBERTS, 20 Sep 1839, Isaac Roberts, adminr.

JOHN LENTZ, Whitemarsh, 17 Sep 1839, Joseph Lentz, Samuel Streeper, Elizabeth Lentz, adminrs.

JOHN SCOTT, Lower Providence, 23 Sep 1839, Christian Dettera, adminr.

JAMES IRWIN, Whitemarsh, 7 Oct 1839, Jonathan Jones, Jr., adminr.

AMOS GODSHALL, Hatfield, 7 Oct 1839, Henry Overholtzer, John Drake, adminrs.

GEORGE WOOL, Whitpain, 16 Oct 1839, Adam Kneedler, adminr.

JOHN CRATER, Upper Providence, 21 Oct 1839, Henry R. Rittenhouse, Abraham Crater, adminrs.

HENRY PRIZER, Upper Dublin, 28 Oct 1839, Joseph Royer, adminr.

JACOB HOFFMAN, Upper Merion, 28 Oct 1839, Jacob Hoffman, adminr.

GARRETT STAUFFER, 2 Nov 1839, Dillman S. Spare, adminr.

SARAH NASH, Upper Dublin, 18 Nov 1839, Daniel Nash, adminr.

HARBISON KINTZING, 19 Nov 1839, James Paul, adminr.

ABNER BARLOW, Potts Grove, 2 Dec 1839, Jacob S. Yost, adminr.

ABNER SPENCER, Upper Dublin, 3 Dec 1839, Mary Spencer, Charles Thomas, adminrs.

DAVID UNDERHOFLER, 7 Dec 1839, Jacob Boyer, Abraham Hunsberger, adminrs.

JOHN WARRINGTON, 10 Dec 1839, Sarah Harrison Warrington, adminr.

HENRY HARST, 16 Dec 1839, Philip Harst, adminr.

ABRAHAM WAMPOLE, 18 Dec 1839, Frederick Wampole, adminr.

GEORGE KNUPP, 26 Dec 1839, Ester Knupp, John Osborn, adminrs.

ABRAHAM IREDELL, Horsham, 6 Jan 1840, G. Mitchell, William Penrose, adminrs.

CATHARINE WISSLER, Upper Hanover, 6 Jan 1840, Peter Shelly adminr.

DAVID SHAFER, Whitpain, 13 Jan 1840, William Hamill, adminr.

ELLEN MARPLE, 23 Jan 1840, Isaac Bean, adminr.

JACOB ROSENBERGER, 25 Jan 1840, Daniel Rosenberger, Abraham Gahman, adminrs.

ISAAC MOYER, 27 Jan 1840, Henry Heist, Lawrence Moyer, adminrs.

DR. EVAN G. LESTER, 15 Feb 1840, Evan Jones, adminr.

CHARLES LEIDY, 17 Feb 1840, Henry Leidy, adminr.

PATRICK BRIEN, 20 Feb 1840, Daniel Reigner, adminr.

GEORGE GREENAWALT, 22 Feb 1840, Sarah G. Anthony, Barnard Connor, Jesse Connor, adminrs.

JOSEPH JOHNSON, Upper Providence, 25 Feb 1840, Jacob Johnson, David Bechtell, adminrs.

DAVID THOMAS, 2 Mar 1840, George W. Thomas, adminr.

CHRISTIAN DULL, 7 Mar 1840, Samuel Custer, adminr.

MARGARET JONES, 14 Mar 1840, Charles Jones, adminr.

JAMES SKEEN, 17 Mar 1840, Elijah Skeen, adminr.

RACHEL COATES, 4 Apr 1840, Lindsay Coates, Elizabeth Coates, adminrs.

ELIZABETH SCHNEIDER, Norrristown, 4 Apr 1840, Henry Schneider, adminr.

ANN L. LEAF, 9 Apr 1840, Jacob S. Yost, adminr.

BENJAMIN WEBER, 11 Apr 1840, David Thomas, adminr.

JOHN FREDERICK, 18 Apr 1840, Jonas Fox, adminr.

CATHARINE FRYER, 15 Apr 1840, Peter Fryer, adminr.

CATHARINE CUSTER, 16 Apr 1840, Matthias Brumback, adminr.

JAMES H. WEBB, 20 May 1840, Philip Hahn, adminr.

BENJAMIN H. PRICE, 18 May 1840, Ellis Maris, adminr.

ELIZABETH MESSIMER, 18 May 1840, Joshua Y. Messimer, adminr.

PETER LEVERGOOD, 26 May 1840, Magdalena Levergood, adminr.

ANN WEBB 28 May 1840, Philip Hahn, adminr.

EDITH FRONEFIELD, Lower Providence, 29 May 1840, John Fronefield, adminr.

DAVID BOLTON, New Hanover, 1 Jun 1840, Thomas Shauer, adminr.

ROBERT EVANS, 6 Jun 1840, Ann Evans, Thomas B. Evans, adminrs.

PETER HENDRICKS, 8 Jun 1840, John Hendricks, Aaron, Linderman, John Christian, adminrs.

JOHN GILBERT, 9 Jun 1840, John Gilbert, Daniel Gilbert, George Bickel, adminrs.

SENECA RADCLIFF, 15 Jun 1840, Rachel Radcliff, Cyrus Radcliff, adminrs.

ESTHER BECHTEL, Potts Grove, 20 Jun 1840, George P. Bechtel, adminr.

JACOB CROLL, Douglass, 2 Jul 1840, Philip Croll, Benjamin Reiff, adminrs.

ISAAC SNYDER, 21 Jul 1840, Teany Snyder, Jacob Ruth, adminrs.

WILLIAM BEAN, 27 Jul 1840, Samuel Sharpe, adminr.

JOHN GISTOCK, 31 Jul 1840, Elizabeth Gistock, William Gistock, adminrs.

HENRY MASSOR, 8 Aug 1840, Philip Sauer, adminr.

ABRAHAM LANDIS, 10 Aug 1840, John Landis, adminr.

ABRAHAM BECHTELL, Upper Providence, 17 Aug 1840, David Bechtell, Henry Bechtell, adminrs.

ROBERT EDWARDS, 17 Aug 1840, Martha Edwards, John Edwards, adminrs.

JACOB METZ, 17 Aug 1840, Garrett Metz, adminr.

DANIEL SCHWENK, 18 Aug 1840, Mary Schwenk, Ephraim A. Schwenk, adminrs.

JANE SAMPEY, 19 Aug 1840, Frederick Wampole, adminr.

HIRAM RAMBO, 19 Aug 1840, David Rambo, adminr.

ADAM SCHRACK, 31 Aug 1840, Adam Schrack, Michael Schrack, adminrs.

JOSEPH DETWILER, Sr., 9 Sep 1840, Jacob Detwiler, Joseph Detwiler, adminrs.

HUGH TARRENCE, 10 Sep 1840, George Tarrence, adminr.

ISAAC OVERHOLTZER, 10 Sep 1840, Daniel Cassel, Abraham Overholtzer, adminrs.

MAGDALENA WHISLER, 12 Sep 1840, Isaac Whisler, Benjamin Rosenberger, adminrs.

ADAM OTTINGER, 14 Sep 1840, Charles Heist, George Dotts, adminrs.

JOHN GROFF, 15 Sep 1840, Christian Sauder, adminr.

REV. GEORGE ROETLER, 29 Sep 1840, Jessias Roetler, Peter Nael, adminrs.

JOHN BOYER, 6 Oct 1840, Eve Boyer, John Thompson, adminrs.

PHILIP KNEEZEL, 7 Oct 1840, Jesse Kneezel, adminr.

ANN CHAIN, 13 Oct 1840, James Chain, Mark Chain, adminrs.

ELIZABETH VANFOSSEN, 16 Oct 1840, James Keel, adminr.

ELIZABETH KNIGHT, 19 Oct 1840, John Evans, adminr.

MICHAEL STEEVER, 2 Nov 1840, Elizabeth Steever, John Steever, adminrs.

CATHARINE SHIVELEY, 4 Nov 1840, John Hearing adminr.

WILLIAM E. WELLS, 16 Nov 1840, Hepsey Morris Wells, adminr.

ROBERT L. PENNIMAN, 17 Nov 1840, Susan Penniman, Benjamin McClellam, adminrs.

SARAH YERKES, 17 Nov 1840, Joseph Yerkes, adminr.

GEORGE FREYER, 20 Nov 1840, Jacob Nace, adminr.

BENJAMIN T. DUNNET, 23 Nov 1840, Christian Dunnet, Silas Shoemaker, adminrs.

ALFRED D. PRICE, Lower Merion, 30 Nov 1840, Paul Jones, adminr.

MARY SPENCER, 2 Dec 1840, Christian Kleisel, adminr.

JOSEPH CONRAD, 2 Dec 1840, Adam Conrad, John Conrad, William Stockdale, adminrs.

DAVID ESBENSHIP, 5 Dec 1840, Henry Esbenship, adminr.

MARY ROSENBERGER, 5 Jan 1841, John Yocum, adminr.

ELIZABETH MCCLEAN, 9 Jan 1841, John McClean, Isaac L. Shoemaker, adminrs.

MARY YOST, 12 Jan 1841, Abraham Yost, adminr.

CONRAD KEELER, 21 Jan 1841, Amos Reifsnyder, James R. Keeler, adminrs.

SARAH ANN HALLMAN, 22 Jan 1841, John Hobensack, adminr.

ENOCH FRY, 25 Jan 1841, John Fry, Edward Fry, adminrs.

CATHARINE HOMSHER, 25 Jan 1841, Jesse Homsher, adminr.

SAMUEL SPEECE, 25 Jan 1841, Henry Speece, adminr.

WILLIAM LENTZ, 1 Feb 1841, Samuel Streeper, George Lentz, adminrs.

VALENTINE SAYLOR, 4 Feb 1841, Elizabeth Saylor, Samuel Markley, adminrs.

MARY CARR, 8 Feb 1841, Daniel Carr, William Long, adminrs.

THOMAS NINAN, 8 Feb 1841, John Kenderdine, adminr.

ISAAC KRUPP, 9 Feb 1941, Sarah Krupp, adminr.

HENRY SMITH, 25 Feb 1841, Samuel S. Smith, Henry Smith, adminrs.

DAVID WOLMER, 20 Feb 1841, Joseph Thomas, adminr.

MARGARET CLYNER, 25 Feb 1841, Daniel Boorse, adminr.

HENRY SUTCH, 25 Feb 1841, William Sutch, John Sutch, adminrs.

BENJAMIN BEAN, 10 Jan 1842, Samuel Bean, William Bean, Benjamin Bean, adminrs.

MARY NINON, 12 Jan 1841, Joseph Ninon, adminr.

ANNA FISHER, 17 Jan 1842, George Fisher, adminr.

JOHN FREDERICK, 18 Jan 1842, Benjamin Frederick, George Frederick, adminrs.

ELIZABETH GRAVER, 19 Jan 1842, Henry Graver, Charles Hillegass, adminrs.

BENJAMIN TYSON. 20 Jan 1842, Benjamin Tyson, John Swartley, adminrs.

GEORGE BASEMAN, 28 Jan 1842, John Blake, adminr.

HENRY BIREHALL, 3 Feb 1842, Mary Birehall, Nathan Birehall, adminrs.

RICHARD MCKNIGHT, Lower Merion, 18 Feb 1842, Samuel Isett, adminr.

ANN BROADES, Lower Merion, 21 Feb 1842, Jacob Broades, John Colflesh, William Colflesh, adminrs.

LEVI DRESHER, 22 Feb 1842, Oliver Dresher, adminr.

JOHN CADWALDER, 5 Mar 1842, Charles Palmer, adminr.

JOHN LEEDOM, 11 Mar 1842, Charles Leedom, Joseph Leedom, Samuel Leedom, adminrs.

CATHARINE CASSEL, 14 Mar 1842, Yellis Cassel, Henry Cassel, adminrs.

CHRISTIAN HUNSBERGER, 14 Mar 1842, Jonathan Hunsberger, Aaron Hunsberger, adminrs.

HENRY KEELEY, 15 Mar 1842, Martin Hunsberger, adminr.

JACOB GILBERT, 21 Mar 1842, Sarah Gilbert, William Gilbert, John Boyer, adminrs.

HENRY WEISEL, 24 Mar 1842, Joseph Weisel, Henry Eckels, adminrs.

LEWIS WOOLMAN, 26 Mar 1842, Rachel Shaw, John Danehouer, adminrs.

ELIZABETH GILBERT, 28 Mar 1842, John Gilbert, Daniel Gilbert, George Bickel, adminrs.

MARGARET SHOEMAKER, 30 Mar 1842, Thomas Wistar, adminr.

LEWIS JONES, 8 Apr 1842, Edward H. Jones, adminr.

JAMES EVANS, 8 Apr 1842, Thomas Evans, I.W. Evans, adminrs.

DEBORAH SMITH, 16 Apr 1842, Cornelius Smith, adminr.

JOHN CHRISTMAN, 19 Apr 1842, Susanna Christman, Isaac Christman, adminrs.

JONATHAN QUILLMAN, 20 Apr 1842, John Miller, Daniel Quillman, adminrs.

LEWIS SPENCER, 5 May 1842, Elizabeth Spencer, adminr.

MARGARET CRESS, 7 May 1842, Henry Cress, adminr.

HENRY HOOKER, 9 May 1842, Jacob Hanes, John Hooker, adminrs.

SAMUEL MUSSELMAN, 11 May 1842, John Katz, adminr.

SAMUEL MCKAY, 24 May 1842, Catharine McKay, adminr.

SAMUEL YEAKEL, 16 May 1842, Hannah Yeakel, adminr.

BENJAMIN CASSELBERRY, 16 May 1842, Isaac Casselberry, adminr.

SAMUEL LINSINBIGLER, 17 May 1842, Charlotte Linsinbigler, adminr.

JOHN CONRAD, 17 May 1842, John Wilfong, adminr.

JOSHUA PAXSON, 13 Jun 1842, Joseph Paxson, Joshua Paxson, adminrs.

JOHN OTT, 9 Jun 1842, Isaac Roberts, adminr.

JOHN WATERS, 13 Jun 1842, Lewis Waters, adminr.

SUSANNA FOULKE, 9 Jul 1842, Edward Foulke, adminr.

JACOB HIGHLEY, 20 Jul 1842, Sarah Highley, John Highler, Jacob Highler, adminrs.

AARON MEREDITH, 30 Jul 1842, Phebe Meredith, adminr.

HENRY HARMAN, 15 Aug 1842, John Harman, adminr.

RINARD MARCH, 15 Aug 1842, Joshua March, adminr.

JOHN ANDERSON, 16 Aug 1842, Sarah Anderson, Jacob Anderson, Jacob Price, adminrs.

NATHANIEL WEASER, 16 Aug 1842, Jonas Smith, adminr.

JOHN SMITH, 26 Aug 1842, Jesse Gable, adminr.

EDWARD JONES, 27 Aug 1842, Christian Jones, Alexander Jones, adminrs.

JAMES BAIRD, 8 Sep 1842, Levina Baird, Christian Snyder, adminrs.

ELIZABETH SCHLATER, 12 Sep 1842, William Schlater, John Schlater, adminrs.

JACOB MINNINGER, 13 Sep 1842, John Katz, adminr.

BAKER BARNES, 22 Sep 1842, Benjamin Barnes, Robert Barnes, adminrs.

JACOB SHULER, 4 Oct 1842, Jacob Fry, adminr.

ISAAC MOORE, 6 Oct 1842, Isaac Eastburn, adminr.

PETER BOORSE, 7 Oct 1842, John Boorse, Daniel Boorse, adminrs.

JOHN AMBERS, 8 Oct 1842, Daniel Foulke, adminr.

GEORGE MAJOR, 13 Oct 1842, Louisa Major, adminr.

THOMAS STACKHOUSE, 17 Oct 1842, Abel Satterthwaite, adminr.

DERRICK HOGELAND, 20 Oct 1842, Richard Hogeland, Sigmond Hogeland, adminrs.

JAMES THOMPSON, 29 Oct 1842, William Thompson, adminr.

JOHN MILLER, 5 Nov 1842, William Miller, John Miller, William Beans, adminrs.

GEORGE LEAF, 14 Nov 1842, Jacob Yost, adminr.

CHRISTINA LEOBOLD, 15 Nov 1842, Wendel Weant, adminr.

SUSANNA LLOYD, 21 Nov 1842, John Lloyd, adminr.

ANN PENNEPACKER, 22 Nov 1842, Jacob Custer, adminr.

JOHN HOFFMAN, 23 Nov 1842, John Hoffman, George Hoffman, adminrs.

SARAH NOBLIT, 23 Nov 1842, Richard Jones, adminr.

SAMUEL MOYER, 3 Dec 1842, Jacob Moyer, John Moyer, adminrs.

JESSE UMSTEAD, Whitpain, 17 Dec 1842, Elizabeth Umstead, adminr.

JANE POLLOCK, 24 Dec 1842, John Shannon, adminr.

JOSEPH GROFF, 28 Dec 1842, Samuel Groff, Abraham Groff, adminrs.

MICHAEL HUBER, 19 Jan 1843, Josiah Huber, Charles Huber, adminrs.

JOHN MATLOCK, 14 Jan 1843, John Katz, adminr.

SOLOMON PHILLIPS, 14 Jan 1843, David Roberts, adminr.

CATHARINE OBERHOLTZER, Lower Salford, 17 Jan 1843, Peter Hunsberger, adminr.

REUBEN WILLIAMS, 20 Jan 1843, George Williams, adminr.

ABRAHAM FRY, 20 Jan 1843, Isaac Christman, adminr.

ANDREW HOFFMAN, 20 Jan 1843, Joseph Hoffman, Andrew Hoffman, adminrs.

DAVID THOMAS, Whitpain, 25 Jan 1843, Joseph Bell, Thomas Bell, John Bell, adminrs.

JOHN SHELMIRE, Moreland, 25 Jan 1843, Elijah Shelmire, Simon Banes, adminrs.

ELLEN DAURELL, Pottstown, 30 Jan 1843, Jacob Yost, adminr.

ABRAHAM KLINE, Lower Salford, 30 Jan 1843, Jacob Kline, Jacob Shutt, adminrs.

WILLIAM YOCUM, Plymouth, 4 Feb 1843, Francis Lyle, adminr.

CHRISTIAN SHUPARD, Whitemarsh, 8 Feb 1843, Margaret Shupard, adminr.

REV. DANIEL HANGER, Upper Providence, 11 Feb 1843, Robert Umstead, adminr.

DAVID KREIBEL, Upper Salford, 16 Feb 1843, Elizabeth Kriebel, Philip Kriebel, Henry Kriebel, adminrs.

PHILLIP HOFFMAN, Lower Merion, 21 Feb 1843, Anthony Anderson, adminr.

JAMES PETERSON, Upper Dublin, 21 Feb 1843, William Jones, adminr.

SUSANNA SEYLOR, Limerick, 21 Feb 1843, Henry Seylor, adminr.

MORDECAI EVANS, Limerick, 22 Feb 1843, Amos Evans, adminr.

WILLIAM VAUGHAN, Norriton, 23 Feb 1843, George Pawling, adminr.

SARAH LUKENS, Abington, 24 Feb 1843, Samuel Shoemaker, adminr.

GEORGE CLEMENS, Lower Salford, 11 Mar 1843, Henry Clemens, Abraham Clemens, adminrs.

LUDWIG MILLER, Limerick, 4 Mar 1843, Henry Brown, John Willauer, adminrs.

JOHN WAMBACH, Pottsgrove, 6 Mar 1843, Bartholomew Wambach, adminr.

FREDERICK SMITH, Frederick, 14 Mar 1843, Benjamin Sheadel, John Steiner, adminrs.

JOHN SMITH, Douglass, 16 Mar 1843, Elizabeth Smith, adminr.

DANIEL BRANT, Whitpain, 18 Mar 1843, Joseph Brant, adminr.

JOHN ALDERFER, Lower Salford, 24 Mar 1843, Margaret Alderfer, Michael Alderfer, adminrs.

MARTIN DETWILER, Whitpain, 27 Mar 1843, Jacob Bean, Jacob Clemens, adminrs.

JOHN MILLER, New Hanover, 30 Mar 1843, Mary Miller, Daniel Miller, adminrs.

MOSES SPENCER, Upper Dublin, 1 Apr 1843, Isaac Witcomb, adminr.

JACOB BARTOLET, Frederick, 3 Apr 1843, Samuel Bartolet, adminr.

GEORGE DEWEES, Whitemarsh, 6 Apr 1843, John Hobensack, adminr.

PHILIP SHENEBERGER, Whitpain, 7 Apr 1843, Conard Booz, adminr.

SARAH WEEK, Abington, 10 Apr 1843, Jonathan Goodwin, adminr.

MARY SHIPE, Hatfield, 10 Apr 1843, Abraham Shipe, Yellis Cassel, adminrs.

WILLIAM SUTCH, Moreland, 11 Apr 1843, John Sutch, Samuel Shoemaker, adminrs.

JACOB KOLP, Whitemarsh, 22 Apr 1843, Mary Kolp, Daniel Kolp, adminrs.

ABRAHAM SCHELLY, Douglass, 25 Apr 1843, Joel Schelly, adminr.

ELIZABETH WEAVER, Frederick, 29 Apr 1843, John Weaver, adminr.

ROBERT HENDERSON, Philadelphia, 1 May 1843, Rachel Smith, Benjamin Hughes, adminrs.

JACOB DE HAVEN, 6 May 1843, Henry De Haven, adminr.

PHILIP ROSHON, Limerick, 9 May 1843, Isaac Roshon, Philip Roshon, adminrs.

ISAAC HOFFMAN, Lower Merion, 11 May 1843, Mary Hoffman, adminr.

THOMAS LEWIS, 13 May 1843, Thomas Lewis, Christian Bates, adminrs.

JOHN BERGEY, Franconia, 22 May 1843, Henry Bergey, Samuel Bergey, adminrs.

ELLWOOD MAULSBY, Whitemarsh, 22 May 1843, Jonathan Mausby, adminr.

JACOB RITTENHOUSE, Upper Providence, 25 May 1843, Henry Rittenhouse, David Rittenhouse, Martin Rittenhouse, adminrs.

JOHN BUCHER, 25 May 1843, Daniel Bucher, adminr.

ABRAHAM FILLMAN, Pottsgrove, 27 May 1843, Israel Fillman, adminr.

ABRAHAM HEEBNER, Norristown, 1 Jun 1843, Elizabeth Heebner, John Heebner, adminrs.

JOSEPH HOLLOWAY, Upper Providence, 2 May 1843, John Holloway, David Holloway, William Holloway, adminrs.

BENJAMIN CONRAD, Whitpain, 21 Jun 1843, Aaron Conrad, Osborn Conrad, adminrs.

ABRAHAM KUHLER, Gwynedd, 5 Jun 1843, Charles Gregor, John Kuhler, adminrs.

JOHN KOLB, Upper Salford, 7 Jun 1843, Isaac Kolb, Jacob Kolb adminrs.

ABRAHAM BERGE, Limerick, 19 Jun 1843, David Berge, Isaac Berge, adminrs.

PHILIP TRUMBOWER, Upper Hanover, 21 Jun 1843, Susanna Trumbower, adminr.

JOSEPH BARTHOLOMEW Limerick, 3 Jul 1843, Isaac Husberger, adminr.

ANN WALTON, Moreland, 11 Jul 1843, Samuel Shoemaker, adminr.

MAHLON KNIPE, Gwynedd, 13 Jul 1843, David Knipe, adminr.

ISAAC GARBER, Upper Providence, 27 Jul 1843, John Hiltebeitel, Henry Rittenhouse, adminrs.

WILLIAM PAWLING, Lower Providence, 7 Aug 1843, John Shearer, John Umstead, adminrs.

CHARLES SENTMAN, Upper Providence, 10 Aug 1843, William Worrell, adminr.

JACOB STOVER, Towamencin, 19 Aug 1843, Henry Stover, adminr.

GEORGE JENKINS, Montgomery, 21 Aug 1843, Levi Jenkins, adminr.

ANN MAGUIRE, Cheltenham, 22 Aug 1843, Isaac Phipps, adminr.

JACOB SPERRY, Gwynedd, 24 Aug 1843, Daniel Foulke, adminr.

DANIEL NYCE, Marlborough, 25 Aug 1843, John Nyce, adminr.

PETER RAMBO, Upper Merion, 4 Sep 1843, Lindsay Coates, adminr.

CHRISTIAN DETWILER, Franconia, 5 Sep 1843, Joseph Detwiler, George Detwiler, adminrs.

HENRY BICKEL, Douglass, 11 Sep 1843, Mary Bickel, adminr.

WILLIAM THOMPSON, Whitemarsh, 16 Sep 1843, Daniel Hitner, adminr.

CHARLES COX, Plymouth, 25 Sep 1843, Daniel Heist, adminr.

MARY TYSON, Abington, 3 Oct 1843, Jonathan Lukens, Edwin Tyson, adminrs.

SIMON SCHNEIDER, Norristown, 4 Oct 1843, Mary Ann Schneider, Henry Schneider, Franklin Derr, adminrs.

JACOB PETERMAN, Providence, 7 Oct 1843, Anthony Sheimer, adminr.

JOHN PERCH, Upper Providence, 14 Oct 1843, Henry Netz, adminr.

MARY DEAL, Plymouth, 16 Oct 1843, John Streeper, Alexander Carson, Catharine Longaker, Mary Davis, adminrs.

DANIEL DEAL, Plymouth, 16 Oct 1843, John Hart, John Streeper, Alexander Carson, Catharine Longaker, Mary Davis, adminrs.

JACOB HUNSBERGER, Hatfield, 28 Oct 1843, John Hunsberger, Isaac Hunsberger, adminrs.

JACOB EDINGER, Whitemarsh, 2 Nov 1843, Francis Kerh, adminr.

BENJAMIN DAVIS, Montgomery, 2 Nov 1843, Jacob Cassel, Thomas Wilson, adminrs.

AMOS ADAMSON, Towamencin, 15 Nov 1843, John Adamson, Reuben Haas, adminrs.

HENRY HALLMAN, Plymouth, 18 Nov 1843, John Hallman, George Hallman, adminrs.

RICHARD KIMBLE, 20 Nov 1843, Isaiah Kimble, Owen Kimble, adminrs.

JOHN MOORE, Upper Merion, 23 Nov 1843, Edwin Moore, adminr.

HENRY MISSIMER, Limerick, 27 Nov 1843, Margaret Missimer, Lewis McAfee, adminrs.

SARAH STREEPER, Whitemarsh, 28 Nov 1843, John Culp, adminr.

HENRY BODEY, Lower Merion, 9 Dec 1843, Lawrence Corson, adminr.

JOSEPH GROFF, Frederick, 14 Dec 1843, Jesse Dabb, adminr.

JAMES THOMPSON, 23 Dec 1843, Daniel O. Hitner, adminr.

JOHN IREDELL, Horsham, 28 Dec 1843, John Iredell, George Iredell, adminrs.

JOHN M. SMITH, Upper Merion, 30 Dec 1843, John Tapper, adminr.

MICHAEL SCHOLL, Franconia, 1 Jan 1844, William Will, George Frederick, adminrs.

MARY RAPINE, Springfield, 4 Jan 1844, Frederick Markley, adminr.

MARY JOHNSON, Abington, 5 Jan 1844, Mark Watson, William Johnson, adminrs.

AMOS THOMAS, Upper Providence, 5 Jan 1844, John Dismant, adminr.

JOHN KRAMER, Franconia, 18 Jan 1843, Elizabeth Kramer, John Brant, adminrs.

SOPHIA FRYER, Douglass, 25 Jan 1844, Samuel Fryer, adminr.

HENRY HUNSICKER, Perkiomen & Skippack, John Hunsicker, Henry Hunsicker, Daniel Hunsicker, adminrs.

JACOB PRICE, Moreland, 31 Jan 1844, Amos Addis, adminr.

ANTHONY FOX, Douglass, 31 Jan 1844, Jonas Fox, James Fox, Reuben Fox, adminrs.

JOHN CASSEL, Skippack & Perkiomen, 1 Feb 1844, Joseph Cassel, Joseph Custer, adminrs.

HANNAH JONES, Cheltenham, 2 Feb 1844, John Brann, Joseph Kenderdine, adminrs.

NOAH GROFF, Frederick, 7 Feb 1844, Isaac Groff, adminr.

JOHN SUPPLEE, Lower Merion, 8 Feb 1844, Abraham Supplee, William Supplee, adminrs.

ABRAHAM JOHNSON, 10 Feb 1844, Elizabeth Johnson, David Bergey, adminrs.

JOSEPH JOHNSON, 12 Feb 1844, Jacob Johnson, William Johnson, adminrs.

JOHN BRITTIN, Abington, 17 Feb 1844, Robert Knight, adminr.

MAGDALENA RAMBO, Upper Merion, 19 Feb 1844, David Rambo, adminr.

ISAAC SCHLICHTER, Hatfield, 19 Feb 1844, Tobias Oberholtzer, adminr.

TOBIAS REIFSNYDER, New Hanover, 20 Feb 1844, Henry Grob, adminr.

CHARLES RAMSEY, Upper Merion, 20 Feb 1844, John Ramsey, Jesse Ramsey, adminrs.

JOHN HURST, Whitpain, 21 Feb 1844, Charles Hurst, adminrs.

MICHAEL WIERMAN, Franconia, 26 Feb 1844, John Freed, adminr.

WILLIAM CRAWFORD, Upper Merion, 27 Feb 1844, Samuel Crawford, Joseph Crawford, adminrs.

HANNAH CLOVER, Moreland, 27 Feb 1844, Charles Stackhouse, adminr.

HENRY HAUCH, Frederick, 1 Mar 1844, Henry Hauch, adminr.

HANNAH SMITH, Gwynedd, 5 Mar 1844, George Danehouer, adminr.

SUSAN JOHNSON, Skippack, 9 Mar 1844, Joseph Johnson, adminr.

JAMES MAGEE, Horsham, 11 Mar 1844, Henry Magee, adminr.

JACOB CASSEL, Skippack & Perkiomen, 12 Mar 1844, Jesse Cassel, adminr.

SAMUEL MCNULDY, New Hanover, 13 Mar 1844, Daniel McNuldy, David McNuldy, adminrs.

JOHN WAMBACH, Pottsgrove, 18 Mar 1844, Bartholomew Wambach, Jacob Wambach, adminrs.

JOHN MCCLEAN, Horsham, 19 Mar 1844, William McClean, adminr.

ADAM FLECK, Gwynedd, 29 Mar 1844, Jacob Hoover, adminr.

ISAAC HALLOWELL, Abington, 2 Apr 1844, Spencer Shoemaker, adminr.

MARY JONES, Norristown, 5 Apr 1844, Mary Kerr, adminr.

GEORGE GESSINGER, Gwynedd, 12 Apr 1844, Henry Hallman, adminr.

PHINEAS BUCKMAN, Abington, 15 Apr 1844, James Buckman, Benjamin Hallowell, adminrs.

JESSE MCCALLA, 15 Apr 1844, Mary McCalla, adminr.

MARY RUMER, Whitpain, 23 Apr 1844, John Rumer, adminr.

JOHN FLECK, Gwynedd, 23 Apr 1844, Adam Fleck, adminr.

ELIZABETH HORN, Lower Merion, 29 Apr 1844, Henry Bevan, adminr.

MICHAEL STUFFLET, Pottsgrove, 3 May 1844, Henry Stufflet, adminr.

JOHN ROSSITER, Norristown, 4 May 1844, John Vanderslice, adminr.

ABRAHAM KRIEBEL, Worcester, 7 May 1844, Joseph Kriebel, George Kriebel, Frederick Schultz, Jeremiah Anders, adminrs.

GEORGE HOWELL, Gwynedd, 11 May 1844, Abner Watson, adminr.

CATHARINE WILSON, Upper Dublin, 11 May 1844, Joseph Wilson, Charles Wilson, adminrs.

SUSANNA HILLEGASS, Frederick, 11 May 1844, Daniel Smith, adminr.

NATHAN DE HAVEN, Upper Merion, 15 May 1844, Nathan Rambo, adminr.

JOHN LENTZ, Whitemarsh, 16 May 1844, John Lentz, Elizabeth Lentz, adminrs.

JOHN LUKENS, Towamencin, 21 May 1844, Jesse Harner, adminr.

SUSANNA ZIMMERMAN, Norriton, May 1844, William Rittenhouse, Henry Rhoads, Charles Rhoads, William Rhoads, John Baird, adminrs.

REBECCA CUSTER, Upper Providence, 29 May 1844, Daniel Custer, adminr.

JOHN CASSEL, Worcester, 4 Jun 1844, Samuel Cassel, adminr.

JOHN HOCKER, Whitemarsh, 5 Jun 1844, Elizabeth Hocker, Martin Hocker, John Jones, adminrs.

THOMAS WHITE, Plymouth, 6 Jun 1844, John Zimmerman, John Cowden, adminrs.

JACOB YOUNG, Douglass, 8 Jun 1844, Sarah Young, Andrew Hoffman, adminrs.

JOSEPH MATHER, Whitemarsh, 17 Jun 1844, Joseph Mather, Allan Corson, adminrs.

SARAH HENDRICKS, 26 Feb 1841, Abraham Hendricks, John Cassel, adminrs.

JOHN FONTOLET, 1 Mar 1841, William Powel, adminr.

THOMAS MYERS, 1 Mar 1841, George D. Price, adminr.

JACOB LICK, 16 Mar 1841, John Lick, adminr.

MAGDALENA KNELL, 24 Mar 1841, Charles Corson, adminr.

JOHN NEIMAN, 29 Mar 1841, Joseph Neiman, John Neiman, adminrs.

ELIZABETH YEAKLE, 13 Mar 1841, Evan Jones, adminr.

JOHN W. BIGONY, 6 Apr 1841, Joseph Bigony, adminr.

JOHN HARMAN, 7 Apr 1841, George M. Potts, adminr.

ABRAHAM ZIGLER, 13 Apr 1841, John Zigler, Michael Zigler, Henry Fryer, adminrs.

VALENTINE KEELY, 16 Apr 1841, Valentine Keely, Benjamin Keely, adminrs.

MICHAEL DRACE, 24 Apr 1841, Peter Drace, Abraham Drace, adminrs.

MARY SPECE, 17 May 1841, Henry Spece, adminr.

PETER SCHOLL, 19 May 1841, Michael Scholl, adminr.

CHRISTIAN MOYER, Upper Salford, 20 May 1841, Jacob Moyer, Abraham Moyer, adminrs.

ISAAC MORE, 2 Jun 1841, Wells Moore, Isaac Eastburn, adminrs.

MARY LEIDY, 3 Jun 1841, Aaron Leidy, Isaiah W. Leidy, adminrs.

JANE LLEWELLYN, 9 Jun 1841, Samuel L. Robinson, adminr.

JOHN HUGHES, 9 Jun 1841, George Roberts, adminr.

ARCHIBALD D. CRAWFORD, 11 Jun 1841, Samuel Crawford, adminr.

WILLIAM MINTZER, 15 Jun 1841, Sarah Mintzer, John H. Hobart, William Mintzer, adminrs.

LYDIA WAGER, 19 Jun 1841, Jacob Wager, adminr.

EDITH GILKESON, 21 Jun 1841, Edward Burke, adminr.

WILLIAM JONES, 29 Jun 1841, David Jones, adminr.

CATHARINE KNEEDLER, 26 Jul 1841, Joseph Kneedler, adminr.

JOHN WEILER, 26 Jul 1841, John S. Weiler, adminr.

DAVID GAULDEY, 28 Jul 1841, Matthias Brumback, adminr.

ELIZABETH DANNEHOWER, 3 Aug 1841, Jacob Dannehower, John Griffin, adminrs.

JACOB MOYER, Lower Salford, 17 Aug 1841, Abraham Moyer, Jacob D. Moyer, adminrs.

THOMAS POTTS, 17 Aug 1841, Thomas Potts, Ephraim Fenton, adminrs.

JAMES ST. CLAIR, 26 Aug 1841, Julia St. Clair, adminr.

JEHU BROOKE, 30 Aug 1841, Samuel Brooke, John Brooke, Adam Brooke, adminrs.

HENRY JOHNSON, 20 Sep 1841, Laurence E. Corson, adminr.

CHRISTIAN TEANY, 23 Sep 1841, Jacob Teany, Benjamin Teany, adminrs.

ANTHONY MCINTIRE, 25 Sep 1841, James McGlinekey, adminr.

JOHN MACK, 27 Sep 1841, Sarah Mack, adminr.

MICHAEL MCNARNCE, 30 Sep 1841, John McNarnce, adminr.

JOHN KIRK, 1 Oct 1841, Elias Kirk, Leneia L. Kirk, Thomas Hallowell, adminrs.

ELIZABETH FILE, 15 Oct 1841, Addison May, adminr.

ABRAHAM FREED, 18 Oct 1841, Isaac Freed, Samuel Souder, adminrs.

SAMUEL H. TRAUER, 20 Oct 1841, John Seltzer, adminr.

MARY NINON, 1 Nov 1841, John Kinderdine, adminr.

ROBERT CAMPBELL, 1 Nov 1841, Mehelm McGlathery, adminr.

GEORGE EGBERT, 3 Nov 1841, Joseph Kirkner, adminr.

CASPER LAYMAN, 10 Nov 1841, William Layman, William Carver, adminrs.

THOMAS ELY, 16 Nov 1841, George M. Potts, adminr.

HENRY GROBB, 22 Nov 1841, Henry S. Groff, Jacob Snyder, adminrs.

JAMES WHITE, Jr., 24 Nov 1841, John White, adminr.

JOHN RUDY, 20 Dec 1841, Jesse Rudy, adminr.

CASPER ESCLINE, 30 Dec 1841, John M. Hunsicker, adminr.

BENJAMIN BEAN, 10 Jan 1842, Samuel Bean, William Bean, Benjamin Bean, adminrs.

BENJAMIN KRIEBLE, Lower Salford, 24 Jun 1844, Samuel Krieble, adminrs.

MICHAEL ALLABACH, Providence, 6 Jul 1844, John Allabach, David Allabach, Henry Allabach, Thomas Casselberry, adminrs.

HENRY WALD, Limerick, 12 Jul 1844, Henry Wald, Peter Wald, adminrs.

PATRICK MCGOWAN, Lower Merion, 19 Jul 1844, Sarah McGowan, adminr.

GEORGE BAIRD, Norristown, 20 Jul 1844, James Baird, adminr.

HENRY KRIER, Moreland, 22 Jul 1844, Mahlon McGlathery, adminr.

JOSEPH THOMAS, Norristown, 23 Jul 1844, Margaret Thomas, Evan Jones, Addison May, adminrs.

MARIA LATSHAW, Pottsgrove, 24 Jul 1844, Jacob Latshaw, adminr.

MARY MARTIN, Worcester, 27 Jul 1844, Sarah Martin, adminr.

KEZIAH HENDERSON, Upper Merion, 27 Jul 1844, Robert Tyson, adminr.

HANNAH JOHNSON, Moreland, 29 Jul 1844, John Finney, Gilliam Cornell, adminrs.

HENRY PRUNER, Gwynedd, 7 Aug 1844, Jacob Pruner, adminr.

HENRY STETLER, Douglass, 10 Aug 1844, Maria Stetler, adminr.

ISRAEL SCHULTZ, Worcester, 12 Aug 1844, Anthony Heebner, George Schultz, adminrs.

RUTH WARNER, Moreland, 17 Aug 1844, Mary Warner, adminr.

JOHN NYCE, Marlborough, 19 Aug 1844, Samuel Nyce, adminr.

ALBAN FREE, Lower Merion, 19 Aug 1844, Lewis J. Free, adminr.

ELIZABETH ESTERLINE, Frederick, 19 Aug 1844, Frederick Smith, adminr.

ADAM RINEWALT, Providence, 19 Aug 1844, Jacob Reazor, adminr.

NOAH HALDEMAN, Douglass, 19 Aug 1844, Susanna Haldeman, adminr.

PETER MATTIS, Plymouth, 20 Aug 1844, Henry Argue, adminr.

ELIAS YERKES, Moreland, 20 Aug 1844, Samuel Lukens, adminr.

SAMUEL THOMAS, Whitpain, 27 Aug 1844, John Bell, adminr.

WILLIAM HODGE, Norriton, 27 Aug 1844, Samuel McKinney, adminr.

JOSEPH ARMSTRONG, Upper Merion, 30 Aug 1844, Benjamin Armstrong, adminr.

ELIZABETH COLER, Whitemarsh, 2 Sep 1844, Abraham Dull, adminr.

CHRISTOPHER LENTZ, Springfield, 4 Sep 1844, Henry Lentz, adminr.

PAUL COPE Hatfield, 6 Sep 1844, Adam Cope, Michael Furhman, adminrs.

LEVI WENTZ, Upper Dublin, 9 Sep 1844, Charles Wentz, Emanuel Wentz, adminrs.

GEORGE DELP, Franconia, 10 Sep 1844, Susanna Delp, adminr.

DAVID UMSTEAD, Frederick, 10 Sep 1844, Salathiel Umstead, adminr.

DOROTHEA MCCALLA, 11 Sep 1844, Alexander McCalla, adminr.

WILLIAM BRANDT, Limerick, 11 Sep 1844, Catharine Brandt, adminr.

JACOB KEPNER, Pottsgrove, 14 Sep 1844, William Kepner, adminr.

WILLIAM FITZWATER, Norriton, 18 Sep 1844, Jonathan Pugh, Ellis Pugh, Samuel Pugh, adminrs.

JOHN ROSEN, Worcester, 18 Sep 1844, Isaac Rosen, adminr.

AARON KEECH, Lower Merion, 28 Sep 1844, Henry Keech, adminr.

THOMAS MAXWELL, Lower Merion, 30 Sep 1844, Thomas Maxwell, adminr.

BENJAMIN ANDERS, Worcester, 30 Sep 1844, Anthony Heebner, George Schultz, adminrs.

JOHN HUNSBERGER, Hatfield, 4 Oct 1844, Sarah Hunsberger, adminr.

NATHANIEL BARNS, Moreland, 10 Oct 1844, Samuel Shoemaker, adminr.

DANIEL SCHEETZ, Norriton, 10 Oct 1844, Sarah Scheetz, Jacob Scheetz, adminrs.

JOHN SHEARER, Whitpain, 12 Oct 1844, John Shearer, George Williams, adminrs.

JOHN LANDIS, 14 Oct 1844, John Eckerd, adminr.

JOHN ADAM FAVINGER, Providence, 17 Oct 1844, John Lehman, adminr.

MARY BEAN, Skippack & Perkiomen, 19 Oct 1844, John Bean, adminr.

PETER LAVER, Pottsgrove, 23 Oct 1844, Michael Engle, adminr.

SAMUEL HUMPHREYS, Lower Merion, 24 Oct 1844, Benjamin Humphreys, adminr.

MARGARET DOTTS, Whitemarsh, 25 Oct 1844, John Hobensack, adminr.

JACOB DANEHOWER, Gwynedd, 4 Nov 1844, Catharine Danehower, Charles Danehower, George Danehower, Rowland Danehower, Adam Fleck, adminrs.

ANNA PASS, Whitemarsh, 5 Nov 1844, John Katz, adminr.

JACOB HOOVER, Gwynedd, 9 Nov 1844, John Hoover, Adam Hoover, Jacob Hoover, adminrs.

CATHARINE FETZER, Whitpain, 11 Nov 1844, William Fetzer, adminr.

FREDERICK ZEARFOSS, Whitpain, 11 Nov 1844, Benjamin Zearfoss, John Sheneberger, adminrs.

CATHARINE REX, Moreland, 21 Nov 1844, George Rex, John Rex, adminrs.

ANTHONY WILLIAMS, Abington, 21 Nov 1844, Charles Thompson, William Thompson, John Thompson, adminrs.

DENNIS SHOEMAKER, Gwynedd, 25 Nov 1844, Thomas Shoemaker, adminr.

JOHN HENDRICKS, Limerick, 4 Dec 1844, Daniel Hendricks, Peter Hendricks, adminrs.

JONAS MOYER, Limerick, 4 Dec 1844, Daniel Geiger, adminr.

PETER HAUBERGER, New Hanover, 19 Dec 1844, Jonas Hauberger, adminr.

ABRAHAM BREY, Marlborough, 26 Dec 1844, George Brey, Isaac Stull, adminrs.

HENRY BOWMAN, New Hanover, 31 Dec 1844, William Specht, adminr.

CATHARINE CASSEL, Lower Salford, 31 Dec 1844, Samuel Cassel, adminr.

ELIZABETH HENDRICKS, Limerick, 1 Jan 1845, Aaron Linderman, John Christman, adminrs.

JACOB KOCH, Douglass, 1 Jan 1845, Jonas Koch, George Koch, adminrs.

SAMUEL WETHERILL, Lower Providence, 9 Jan 1845, Charlotte Wetherill, adminr.

TACY CHILDS, Lower Merion, 10 Jan 1845, Joseph Conrad, adminr.

SAMUEL JACOBY, Plymouth, 15 Jan 1845, Susanna Jacoby, adminr.

GEORGE MALSBERGER, Pottstown, 15 Jan 1845, John Rowan, adminr.

PHILEPENA YERGE, New Hanover, 15 Jan 1845, John Yerge, adminr.

SAMUEL HARVEY, Abington, 20 Jan 1845, Elizabeth Harvey, adminr.

JOSEPH LEEDOM, Plymouth, 22 Jan 1845, Eleanor Leedom, Daniel Mulvaney, adminrs.

JOSEPH LENHART, Cheltenham, 24 Jan 1845, John Lenhart, David Heist, adminrs.

JOHN BINDER, New Hanover, 27 Jan 1845, William Binder, Jacob Binder, adminrs.

ELIZABETH AXE, Norristown, 27 Jan 1845, John McKay, George Wright, adminrs.

MARY LAYMAN, Gwynedd, 3 Feb 1845, Evan Jones, Lewis Jones, adminrs.

JOHN HISER, Lower Providence, 11 Feb 1845, Henry Hiser, John Hiser, John Saylor, adminrs.

JOHN BEAN, Norristown, 17 Feb 1845, Benjamin Chain, adminr.

PHILIP MARKLEY, Skippack & Perkiomen, 18 Feb 1845, Abraham Markley, Jacob Markley, Philip Markley, adminrs.

ELIZABETH EDWARDS, Upper Providence, 7 Mar 1845, John Edwards, adminr.

ABRAHAM LUKENS, Upper Dublin, 8 Mar 1845, Jacob Fitzwater, adminr.

AARON CASSEL, Skippack & Perkiomen, 11 Mar 1845, Benjamin Cassel, adminr.

DANIEL CHRISTMAN, Pottsgrove, 11 Mar 1845, Jacob Christman, Matthew Evans, adminrs.

CHARLES TYSON, Abington, 19 Mar 1845, George Hamell, adminr.

CATHARINE WEIKLE, Lower Salford, 22 Mar 1845, Henry Weikle, adminr.

SARAH ESBENSHIP, Upper Providence, 22 Mar 1845, Henry Esbenship, adminr.

WILLIAM DEWEES, Whitemarsh, 26 Mar 1845, Daniel Dewees, adminr.

HENRY DEWEES, Whitemarsh, 26 Mar 1845, Henry Dewees, adminr.

CHARLES DRAKE, Upper Merion, 28 Mar 1845, Elijah Drake, adminr.

HARMAN YERKES, Whitemarsh, 29 Mar 1845, Joseph Yerkes, Reuben Yerkes, Nathaniel Yerkes, Daniel Dager, adminrs.

JACOB HEISLER, Gwynedd, 1 Apr 1845, Henry Kneedler, adminr.

MARY IREDELL, Norristown, 3 Apr 1845, Acero Hunt, adminr.

HENRY NEWBERRY, Worcester, 5 Apr 1845, John Newberry, Thomas Lewis, adminrs.

EZEKIEL RHOADS, Norriton, 7 Apr 1845, Lydia Rhoads, William Rhoads, adminrs.

ISAAC OBERHOLTZER, Hatfield, 12 Apr 1845, Elizabeth Oberholtzer, Tobias Oberholtzer, adminrs.

PETER MUNSHOWER, Norriton, 12 Apr 1845, Robert Stinson, adminr.

BENJAMIN KUGLER, Lower Providence, 12 Apr 1845, Matthias Yost, adminr.

JOHN HILDEBEITEL, Frederick, 15 Apr 1845, Richard Hollowbush, adminr.

JACOB LONGAKER, Lower Providence, 19 Apr 1845, Henry Longaker, adminr.

WILLIAM OXENFOOT, Douglass, 22 Apr 1844, Elizabeth Oxenfoot, adminr.

JACOB KINSEY, Lower Salford, 2 May 1845, Jacob Kinsey, John Kinsey, adminrs.

BENJAMIN BRANT, Pottsgrove, 7 May 1845, Samuel Brant, George Brant, adminrs.

PHEBE BANES, Moreland, 8 May 1845, Adolph Yerkes, adminr.

WILLIAM DANES, Hatfield, 12 May 1845, Thomas White, John Jenkins, adminrs.

ABRAHAM ZERN, New Hanover, 19 May 1845, John Zern, adminr.

MARTIN NOTTE, Hatfield, 19 May 1845, John Kindig, adminr.

HENRY DAUB, Frederick 19 May 1845, Maria Daub, Daniel Daub, adminrs.

JOHN GARBER, Upper Hanover, 19 May 1845, Christina Garber, William Garber, adminrs.

EDWARD ZOLLER, Skippack, 26 May 1845, Maria Zoller, Isaac Christman, adminrs.

JOHN PIERCE, Upper Dublin, 26 May 1845, Samuel Pierce, Jacob Fitzwater, adminrs.

JACOB THOMAS, Moreland, 4 Jun 1845, Samuel Shoemaker, adminr.

HENRY KEELEY, Whitemarsh, 5 Jun 1845, Rebecca Thomas, Samuel Keeley, adminrs.

JACOB HUNSICKER, Skippack & Perkiomen, 9 Jun 1845, Garret Hunsicker, Abraham Hunsicker, John Hunsicker, adminrs.

GEORGE STAUDT, Upper Hanover, 11 Jun 1845, John Staudt, adminr.

JACOB SCHWENK, Gwynedd, 24 Jun 1845, Aaron Schwenk, Christian Markley, Jacob Pruner, adminrs.

THOMAS FISHER, Moreland, 2 Jul 1845, Joseph Yerkes, adminr.

LEVI CUSTER, Lower Providence, 9 Jul 1845, Joseph Shrawder, adminr.

MARY TYSON, Abington, 14 Jul 1845, Peter Tyson, adminr.

MARY WIERMAN, Hatfield, 22 Jul 1845, Enos Leidy, adminr.

GEORGE HALLMAN, Plymouth, 25 Jul 1845, George Potts, adminr.

MARTIN BURK, Lower Merion, 25 Jul 1845, Mary Burk, adminr.

GEORGE SCHWENK, Limerick, 29 Jul 1845, Abraham Schwenk, Jacob Saylor, adminrs.

WILLIAM WILLARD, Moreland, 29 Jul 1845, Samuel Shoemaker, adminr.

SARAH SHOEMAKER, Cheltenham, 29 Jul 1845, Richard Shoemaker, Samuel Shoemaker, Comly Shoemaker, adminrs.

JOHN HULME, Lower Merion, 5 Aug 1845, John Hulme, Frederick Porter, adminrs.

SAMUEL NASH, Upper Dublin, 11 Aug 1845, Elizabeth Nash, Jacob Fitzwater, adminrs.

SUSANNA ERB, New Hanover, 18 Aug 1845, George Erb, adminr.

CATHARINE HOUPT, Upper Dublin, 19 Aug 1845, Isaac Witcomb, adminr.

WILLIAM PENNICK, Abington, 19 Aug 1845, George Berrell, adminr.

BENJAMIN WEBER, Worcester, 22 Aug 1845, Andrew Lewis, adminr.

ANN STEWART, Upper Merion, 22 Aug 1845, Anderson Stewart, Charles Stewart, adminrs.

MARY LESSIG, Pottstown, 22 Aug 1845, Thomas Reifsnyder, adminr.

ABRAHAM KRUPP, Worcester, 29 Aug 1845, Philip Harley, adminr.

PETER HOUCK, Worcester, 8 Sep 1845, William Cassel, adminr.

JOHN RICHIE, Upper Merion, 10 Sep 1845, Thomas Richie, adminr.

DAVID GEORGE, Upper Dublin, 5 Sep 1845, Ephraim Fenton, adminr.

JOHN NELSON, Frederick, 26 Sep 1845, Elizabeth Nelson, John Steiner, adminrs.

JOHN STOTT, Springfield, 26 Sep 1845, Peter Stott, adminr.

GEORGE DEITRICK, Pottstown, 1 Oct 1845, John Thompson, adminr.

KENDERDINE GORDON, Upper Merion, 16 Oct 1845, Ann Gordon, Dennis Conard, adminrs.

SAMUEL SHOEMAKER, Moreland 17 Oct 1845, Seneca Lukens, John Smith, George Spencer, adminrs.

SAMUEL WAMPOLE, Upper Salford, 20 Oct 1845, Mary Ann Wampole, adminr.

ABIGAIL STINNECKE, Lower Merion, 23 Oct 1845, John Sterigere, adminr.

ANNA NEIMAN, Limerick, 25 Oct 1845, Israel Neiman, adminr.

JACOB RORER, Cheltenham, 4 Nov 1845, Robert Buckman, adminr.

HENRY BOLLAND, Springfield, Nov 1845, William Shugard, Samuel Rex, adminrs.

DANIEL MILLER, New Hanover, 17 Nov 1845, George Miller, adminr.

WILLIAM WILLARD, Moreland, 17 Nov 1845, John Byerly, adminr.

JACOB THOMAS, Moreland, 17 Nov 1845, John Smith, adminr.

HENRY BRANDT, Franconia, 18 Nov 1845, John Brandt, adminr.

ANTHONY ZELL, Lower Merion, 18 Nov 1845, Susanna Zell, Thomas Zell, adminrs.

ISAAC HARDING, Moreland, 18 Nov 1845, Catharine Harding, adminr.

JACOB LONGACRE, Lower Providence, 19 Nov 1845, David Rosenberger, adminr.

MICHAEL LAND, Whitpain, 23 Dec 1845, Rachel Land, Stephen Lewry, adminrs.

CHARLES FILLMAN, Springfield, 27 Dec 1845, John Katz, adminr.

GEORGE WERKISER, Whitpain, 6 Jan 1846, Charles Slingluff, Peter Yost, adminrs.

CATHARINE SUPPLEE, Upper Merion, 10 Jan 1846, Abraham Supplee, adminr.

JOHN DERON, Horsham, 12 Jan 1846, Catharine Deron, adminr.

MARY GEIST, Pottstown, 15 Jan 1846, Henry Geist, adminr.

JACOB FREES, Lower Providence, 15 Jan 1846, Lorenzo Frees, Christian Miller, adminrs.

PETER BRENDLINGER, Douglass, 28 Jan 1846, Daniel Brendlinger, Solomon Brendlinger, adminrs.

PETER LIEBENGUTH, Pottstown, 28 Jan 1846, Sarah Liebenguth, adminr.

ABRAHAM GARIGUS, Lower Salford, 30 Jan 1846, Leah Garigus, Jacob Price, adminrs.

JACOB SHADE, Upper Providence, 2 Feb 1846, Uriah B. Shade, adminr.

BARBARA ERDMAN, Franconia, 10 Feb 1846, Jacob Sloop, adminr.

JOHN DRAKE, Norristown, 11 Feb 1846, Samuel Shaw, Samuel Pennepacker, adminrs.

JOHN FRY, Limerick, 16 Feb 1846, Peter Fry, Henry Fry, adminrs.

LYDIA HOOD, Skippack & Perkiomen, 16 Feb 1846, James Bortman, adminr.

NATHANIEL BARNES, Moreland, 18 Feb 1846, John Smith, adminr.

HENRY MOSER, Worcester, 31 Mar 1846, Jacob Moser, John Beideman, adminrs.

BARBARA KUGLER, Worcester, 5 Mar 1846, Matthias Yost, adminr.

JOHN SUMMERFIELD, Lower Providence, 7 Mar 1846, Benjamin Summerfield, adminr.

SAMUEL GROCE, Gwynedd, 9 Mar 1846, Henry Jordon, adminr.

PETER FEGLEY, Douglass, 11 Mar 1846, Elizabeth Fegley, George Fegley, adminrs.

ANNA CLEMENS, Worcester, 12 Mar 1846, Jacob Clemens, adminr.

JAMES WALTON, 13 Mar 1846, Atkinson Hughs, adminr.

ELIZABETH BERGE, Lower Salford, 18 Mar 1846, David Berge, adminr.

MARY LANDIS, Franconia, 19 Mar 1846, Henry Landis, adminr.

MICHAEL GERY, Upper Hanover, 19 Mar 1846, Joseph Gery, Henry Gery, adminrs.

JACOB WARNER, Upper Providence, 21 Mar 1846, Ann Warner, David Derricks, adminrs.

ISAIAH WALTON, Moreland, 23 Mar 1846, Seth Walton, Joseph Walton, Jacob Walton, Thomas Walton, adminrs.

HANNAH MOORE, 23 Mar 1846, Isaac Jarrett, adminr.

JOSEPH BROADES, Lower Merion, 24 Mar 1846, George Pechin, William Colflesh, adminrs.

AARON BEYER, 25 Mar 1846, Lydia Beyer, adminr.

SAMUEL SPARE, Upper Providence, 28 Mar 1846, John Spare, adminr.

MARGARET BARR, Lower Merion, 28 Mar 1846, Ellis Ramsey, adminr.

ISAAC MORRIS, 6 Apr 1846, Henry Morris, Isaac Rittenhouse, adminr.

HENRY MISSIMER, Pottstown, 7 Apr 1846, Frederick Missimer, adminr.

RICHARD MILLER, Upper Providence, 8 Apr 1846, Catharine Miller, adminr.

HENRY HOFFMAN, New Hanover, 10 Apr 1846, John Erb, adminr.

ANDREW ERDMAN, Upper Salford, 14 Apr 1846, Solomon Artman, adminr.

CATHARINE SCHWENK, Upper Salford, 10 Apr 1846, Charles Schwenk, adminr.

GEORGE GERHART, Upper Salford, 17 Apr 1846, John Gerhart, Enos Gerhart, adminrs.

ROBERT HALLOWELL, Upper Merion, 18 Apr 1846, Sarah Hallowell, Reuben Y. Ramsey, adminrs.

JOHN OTNER, Worcester, 20 Apr 1846, Catharine Otner, Andrew Anders, adminrs.

RACHEL MCDOWELL, 21 Apr 1846, Samuel McClennen, adminr.

JACOB KRAUSE, Limerick, 5 May 1846, Samuel Krause, Daniel Krause, adminrs.

THOMAS JOLLY, 8 May 1846, Rachel Jolly, adminr.

ELIZABETH DAVIS, Upper Providence, 13 May 1846, James Davis, adminr.

GEORGE PHIPPS, Whitpain, 25 May 1846, William Powell, adminr.

JACOB RENNINGER, New Hanover, 26 May 1846, David Sassaman, adminr.

MATTHEW ROBERTS, Upper Merion, 1 Jun 1846, Jonathan Roberts, Mordecai Moore, adminrs.

WILLIAM SHAFFER, Upper Dublin, 1 Jun 1846, George Williams, adminr.

MILES DAVIS, Norristown, 3 Jun 1846, George Davis, William Bartolet, adminrs.

GEORGE WAMBOLDT, Upper Salford, 10 Jun 1846, Abraham Moyer, Abraham Hartzell, adminrs.

JOHN WEBER, Frederick, 1 Jun 1846, Samuel Weber, Ezra Reller, adminrs.

GEORGE MOYER, 11 Jun 1846, Israel Moyer, adminr.

ELIZABETH VANDIKE, Whitemarsh, 6 Jul 1846, Jacob Strouse, adminr.

ANNA FRANTZ, Upper Salford, 20 Jun 1846, John Cramer, adminr.

MARTHA BEARD, Norriton, 23 Jul 1846, John Beard, adminr.

HENRY KINCKINER, Lower Providence, 20 Jul 1846, Philip Kinckiner, John Slough, adminrs.

MARGARET REIFSNYDER, New Hanover, 22 Jul 1846, Deiter Roads, adminr.

ELIZABETH SMITH, New Hanover, 25 Jul 1846, John Smith, adminr.

GEORGE SNELL, Limerick, 1 Aug 1846, Frederick Snell, George Snell, adminrs.

ABRAHAM YOUNG, Lower Salford, 8 Aug 1846, Elizabeth Young, Isaac Young, adminrs.

JOHN SLICHTER, Upper Hanover, 17 Aug 1846, George Slichter, Daniel Slichter, adminrs.

JONATHAN BRIGHT, Abington, 20 Aug 1846, Charles Bright, John Bright, adminrs.

JOHN FRY, Montgomery, 27 Aug 1846, William Fry, John Jenkins, adminrs.

JOHN ASHENFELTER, Upper Providence, 5 Sep 1846, Jonas Ashenfelter, John Ashenfelter, adminrs.

CONARD STONG, Horsham, 10 Sep 1846, Isaac Stong, Philip Stong, adminrs.

THOMAS COULSTON, Lower Providence, 12 Sep 1846, Edward Coulston, adminr.

JOHN ZELL, Lower Merion, 17 Sep 1846, Joseph Trasel, adminr.

ISAAC SHOEMAKER, Gwynedd, 21 Sep 1846, John Jenkins, Charles Jenkins, adminrs.

ANDREW BEYER, Norriton, 21 Sep 1846, Samuel Beyer, Henry Beyer, adminrs.

EVE KRAUSS, Upper Hanover, 28 Sep 1846, Joseph Bitting, adminr.

DAVID SCHOLFIELD, Plymouth, 2 Oct 1846, Mary Scholfield, adminr.

THOMAS RILE, Whitpain, 5 Oct 1846, Jacob Fisher, adminr.

SUSANNA DETWILER, Worcester, 8 Oct 1846, Joseph Metz, adminr.

ELIZABETH DONAT, Upper Dublin, 12 Oct 1846, John Donat, Christian Donat, adminrs.

CATHARINE POOL, Skippack, 12 Nov 1846, Daniel Gross, adminr.

JESSE WENTZ, Whitpain, 24 Nov 1846, David Roberts, adminr.

EDWARD BEAN, Norriton, 26 Nov 1846, John Bean, Christian Miller, adminrs.

REUBEN WORMAN, Hatfield, 4 Dec 1846, Michael Sholl, adminr.

ELEANOR CORSON, Norristown, 5 Dec 1846, George Corson, adminr.

CATHARINE POOL, Skippack & Perkiomen, 7 Dec 1846, Abraham Pool, adminr.

WENDEL WEAND, New Hanover, 11 Dec 1846, John Weand, Barned Weand, adminrs.

HENRY GERHART, Hatfield, 15 Dec 1846, Samuel Gerhart, Simon Gerhart, adminrs.

JOHN REED, Marlborough, 18 Dec 1846, Samuel Nyce, adminr.

DANIEL HARRAR, Montgomery, 22 Dec 1846, William Harrar, adminr.

ADAM EGOLF, New Hanover, 1 Jan 1847, John Egolf, Jacob Egolf, adminrs.

PETER NICOM, Whitpain, 6 Jan 1846, John Nicom, adminr.

JOHN FOX, Upper Providence, 9 Jan 1846, Rebecca Fox, adminr.

JOHN ROSENBERGER, Hatfield, 12 Jan 1846, Martin Rosenberger, David Rosenberger, Henry Fretz, adminrs.

JACOB WECHLER, Franconia, 12 Jan 1847, Philip Barndt, adminr.

HENRY SCHULTZ, Whitemarsh, 14 Jan 1847, Jesse Shepard, Samuel Yeakle, adminr.

EDWARD HOXWORTH, Hatfield, 20 Jan 1847, Israel Hoxworth, adminr.

JOHN PAUL, Limerick, 21 Jan 1847, Samuel Paul, adminr.

JOHN BEVAN, Lower Merion, 28 Jan 1847, Henry Bevan, adminr.

ELIZABETH LONGACRE, Upper Providence, 30 Jan 1847, John Longacre, adminr.

JOHN SMITH, Lower Merion, 9 Feb 1847, Margaret Smith, adminr.

CHARLES JONES, Upper Merion, 10 Feb 1847, Lloyd Jones, adminr.

RACHEL OWENS, Hatfield, 11 Feb 1847, William Rosenberger, adminr.

JEMIMA DAVIS, Lower Providence, 15 Feb 1847, Nathan Davis, Jesse Davis, adminrs.

JACOB LOCK, New Hanover 15 Feb 1847, William Specht, adminr.

PETER HECKLER, Lower Salford, 16 Feb 1847, Abraham Heckler, adminr.

ISAAC ERB, Limerick, 17 Feb 1847, David Evans, adminr.

JOSEPH YERKES, Plymouth, 20 Feb 1847, Daniel Dager, Jonathan Jones, adminrs.

REGINA OBERDORF, Douglass, 24 Feb 1847, George Oberdorf, Walter Oberdorf, adminrs.

JOHN BOSSERT, Upper Hanover, 25 Feb 1847, Reuben Bossert, John Bossert, Lewis Bossert, adminrs.

JACOB LEIDICH, Frederick, 1 Mar 1847, Francis Leidich, Henry Yahn, adminrs.

JOHN BUTTESWA, Norriton, 2 Mar 1847, Abraham Brower, Patrick Flynn, adminrs.

LEWIS GARTER, Skippack & Perkiomen, 8 Mar 1847, Abraham Garter, Ellis Garter, adminrs.

FREDERICK WALT, Upper Salford, 15 Mar 1847, Henry Walt, Francis Walt, adminrs.

DAVID DAVIS, Hatfield, 16 Mar 1847, Tobias Cope, adminr.

ROSANNA HARNER, Whitemarsh, 18 Mar 1847, Henry Harner, Samuel Shannon, Moses Peirce, adminrs.

WILLIAM ACUFF, Gwynedd, 20 Mar 1847, Jacob Acuff, Algernon Jenkins, adminrs.

SAMUEL PERRY, Norristown, 1 Apr 1847, Charles Perry, adminr.

JOSEPH RAWN, Limerick, 12 Apr 1847, Samuel Brant, adminr.

JOSEPH RIGHTER, Plymouth, 13 Apr 1847, Elizabeth Righter, adminr.

JOSEPH KENDERDINE, Horsham, 22 Apr 1847, Rebecca Kenderdine, John Kenderdine, adminrs.

HENRY HEEBNER, Gwynedd, 22 Apr 1847, John Heebner, Joel Wiegner, adminrs.

MARGARET BERGY, Lower Salford, 27 Apr 1847, Christian Bergy, adminr.

THOMAS HALLAS, Lower Merion, 24 Apr 1847, George Floyd, adminr.

MARY YNDERKOFFLER, Frederick, 30 Apr 1847, H.B. Hancock, adminr.

ROBERT MCKNIGHT, Lower Merion, 1 May 1847, Martin Bell, adminr.

JOSHUA BECHTEL, Pottsgrove, 10 May 1847, Jacob Thomas, adminr.

WILLIAM SCHWARTZ, Norristown, 17 May 1847, Louisa Schwartz, adminr.

CATHARINE KEYSER, Springfield, 17 May 1847, William Keyser, adminr.

DAVID URFFER, Upper Hanover, 17 May 1847, Daniel Urffer, adminr.

WILLIAM SUTCH, Moreland, 18 May 1847, William Clime, adminr.

JOHN ADAM, Marlborough, 18 May 1847, Catharine Beyshey, adminr.

HANNAH ZELL, Lower Merion, 21 May 1847, Emma Zell, adminr.

HENRY FOX, New Hanover, 25 May 1847, Jonas Smith, adminr.

JACOB ZEPP, Upper Salford, 31 May 1847, John Zepp, adminr.

JACOB HARNER, Upper Dublin, 1 Jun 1847, Daniel Harner, adminr.

SAMUEL MCCANN, Plymouth, 3 Jun 1847, John McCann, adminr.

JOSHUA YERKES, Moreland, 10 Jun 1847, Amos Yerkes, Jonas Yerkes, adminrs.

JOHN HOSSELMAN, Worcester, 11 Jun 1847, Margaret Hosselman, George Schetz, adminrs.

SUSANNA BEAVER, Gwynedd, 11 Jun 1847, Henry Shade, adminr.

MARY LINDENBERGER, Springfield, 12 Jun 1847, Charles Rorer, adminr.

JACOB PENNEBECKER, Lower Providence, 14 Jun 1847, Mary Pennebecker, Allen Corson, adminrs.

CATHARINE KATES, Whitemarsh, 15 Jun 1847, Jacob Kates, Philip Kates, George Lightcap, William Shinkle, adminrs.

GEORGE DAVIS, Norristown, 16 Jun 1847, Addison May, adminr.

SARAH CONRAD, Norriton, 19 Jun 1847, John Conrad, Robert Conrad, adminrs.

SARAH BENNER, Lower Salford, 19 Jun 1847, Elias Benner, Charles Benner, adminrs.

JOSIAH LOWE, Franconia, 22 Jun 1847, Elizabeth Lowe, adminr.

BENJAMIN HUNSICKER, Upper Providence, 3 Jul 1847, Catharine Hunsicker, Reuben Winter, adminrs.

MARTIN KATZ, Whitemarsh, 12 Jul 1847, Nicholas Rapine, adminr.

JOHN LEWIS, Lower Merion, 12 Jul 1847, Silas Jones, John Jones, adminrs.

ANNA BOYD, Whitemarsh, 12 Jul 1847, William Morris, adminr.

JOSEPH KUHNS, Upper Hanover, 19 Jul 1847, John Kuhns, adminr.

JESSE TYSON, Upper Dublin, 21 Jul 1847, Peter Tyson, adminr.

JACOB LANDES, Skippack & Perkiomen, 6 Aug 1847, Jacob Landes, Daniel Landes, adminrs.

ELIZABETH JEANES, Abington, 12 Aug 1847, Seth Kolb, adminr.

JOSEPH MISSIMER, Pottsgrove, 16 Aug 1847, Joshua Cassimer, adminr.

JOHN SMITH, Plymouth, 16 Aug 1847, Elizabeth Smith, adminr.

ANNA STEWART, Upper Merion, 16 Aug 1847, Anderson Stewart, Charles Stewart, adminrs.

JESSE LEWIS, Whitpain, 19 Aug 1847, Andrew Lewis, adminr.

ANNA KRAUSS, Upper Hanover, 23 Aug 1847, Nathan Krauss, Aaron Krauss, adminrs.

JACOB BOYER, Limerick, 31 Aug 1847, Joseph Boyer, adminr.

FREDERICK BARE, Lower Providence, 14 Sep 1847, John Umstead, William Casselberry, adminrs.

HANNAH DAVIS, Lower Merion, 22 Sep 1847, Lydia Davis, adminr.

JOHN DELP, Upper Salford, 24 Sep 1847, Abraham Moyer, adminr.

GILES BRIGGS, Norristown, 25 Sep 1847, Alfred Briggs, adminr.

GEORGE STINSON, Norristown, 27 Sep 1847, Stephen Stinson, adminr.

THOMAS COULSTON, Lower Providence, 27 Sep 1847, Isaac Christman, adminr.

CATHARINE HARLEY, Lower Salford, 28 Sep 1847, Jacob Harley, adminr.

ELIZABETH GOTTSHALK, Frederick, 30 Sep 1847, William Gottshalk, Moses Gottshalk, adminrs.

JOHN BEAN, Moreland, 30 Sep 1847, Martha Bean, adminr.

GEORGE PELTZ, Limerick, 8 Oct 1847, Philip Stearly, Joseph Nettles, adminrs.

WILLIAM SHAFFER, Upper Dublin, 11 Oct 1847, Lewis Shaffer, adminr.

DEBORAH HESS, Norristown, 12 Oct 1847, Sylvester Hess, adminr.

MARGARET REIFSNYDER, New Hanover, 21 Oct 1847, Dieter Rhoads, Catharine Rhoads, adminrs.

WILLIAM DIEHL, Norriton, 2 Nov 1847, Hannah Diehl, Charles Diehl, adminrs.

MARY GREENAWALT, Gwynedd, 27 Oct 1847, Jesse Frantz, adminr.

HUGH CRAWFORD, Plymouth, 1 Nov 1847, Isabella Crawford, adminr.

ISAAC YEAKLE, Springfield, 8 Nov 1847, Rachel Yeakle, Jacob Yeakle, Daniel Yeakle, adminrs.

GRIFFITH MCDERMOTT, Lower Merion, 8 Nov 1847, Joseph Lawrence, adminr.

MICHAEL EGOLF, Pottsgrove, 9 Nov 1847, Adam Egolf, adminr.

JESSE WILDERMUTH, Pottsgrove, 12 Nov 1847, Henry Wildermuth, Levi Wildermuth, adminrs.

JACOB SHULER, Upper Salford, 13 Nov 1847, John Reichet, adminr.

HENRY BORNEMAN, Frederick, 19 Nov 1847, Henry Borneman, John Borneman, adminrs.

MARY SPENCER, Moreland, 22 Nov 1847, George Spencer, adminr.

JOHN KIRKBRIDE, Norristown, 29 Nov 1847, George Potts, adminr.

ANNA SHOEMAKER, Franconia, 11 Dec 1847, John Zeigler, Henry Fryer, adminr.

JOHN BARLOW, Limerick, 18 Dec 1847, James Barlow, Mahlon Barlow, adminrs.

GEORGE HAWKE, Lower Providence, 20 Dec 1847, George Koons, adminr.

MARY LEHMAN, Lower Providence, 20 Dec 1847, John Lehman, adminr.

JOHN HUNSICKER, Perkiomen, 21 Dec 1847, Joseph Hunsicker, Garrett Hunsicker, Henry Hunsicker, adminrs.

MARY GRUBB, Limerick, 22 Dec 1847, Isaac Erb, adminr.

ABRAHAM DETWILER, Lower Providence, 30 Dec 1847, Benjamin Hunsicker, Isaac Detwiler, adminrs.

MARY LOWRY Plymouth, 30 Dec 1847, John Adamson, Reuben Haas, adminrs.

SAMUEL KINDIG, Hatfield, 3 Jan 1848, John Kindig, adminr.

HENRY HAUCK, Douglass, 30 Dec 1847, John Erb, adminr.

JOSEPH PAWLING, Norristown, 30 Dec 1847, Henry Pawling, adminr.

BERNARD FREYER, Lower Salford, 6 Jan 1848, Christian Freyer, Henry Freyer, adminrs.

JACOB FAMOUS, Upper Merion, 6 Jan 1848, William Famous, Hiram Famous, Isaac Famous, adminrs.

JOHN SHANNON, Norriton, 20 Jan 1848, Samuel Shannon, George Shannon, adminrs.

JACOB GOTWALS, Skippack & Perkiomen, 20 Jan 1848, George Detwiler, adminr.

MAGDALENA NICE, Upper Salford, 24 Jan 1848, John Nice, adminr.

CATHARINE MILLER, Norristown, 24 Jan 1848, Isaac Miller, adminr.

MARIA MARKARATER, Upper Hanover, 26 Jan 1848, Michael Reiter, adminr.

JOHN BREY, Marlborough, 31 Jan 1848, Jonas Hillegass, adminr.

HANNAH ROELLER, Upper Salford, 31 Jan 1848, Josiah Roeller, adminr.

CHRISTIAN SHUPPERT, Whitemarsh, 5 Feb 1848, Frederick Haws, adminr.

A. MORRIS, Hatfield, 8 Feb 1848, Henry Matthias, adminr.

GEORGE GOODMAN, Lower Merion, 8 Feb 1848, William Sibley, adminr.

ABRAHAM DETTERA, Upper Providence, 10 Feb 1848, William Casselberry, adminr.

GEORGE FLOYD, Norristown, 16 Feb 1848, Charles Kugler, adminr.

WILLIAM WARD, Norristown, 17 Feb 1848, Lydia J. Ward, adminr.

NICHOLAS SHOEMAKER, Springfield, 19 Feb 1848, Nicholas Shoemaker, adminr.

DAVID SEASHOLTZ, New Hanover, 21 Feb 1848, Joseph Seasholtz, David Seasholtz, adminrs.

FREDERICK GABLE, Upper Salford, 21 Feb 1848, Christianna Gabel, adminr.

SAMUEL KOLB, Limerick, 21 Feb 1848, John Kolb, adminr.

BENJAMIN FRETZ, Douglass, 21 Feb 1848, Catharine Fretz, adminr.

JOHN SAYBOLT, Worcester, 24 Feb 1848, Henry Saybolt, adminr.

ENOS LUKENS, Hatfield, 29 Feb 1848, Sarah Lukens, William Lukens, Isaac Wampole, adminrs.

SARAH KNOX, Norriton, 1 Mar 1848, Thomas Knox, adminr.

TYSON JONES, Abington, 1 Mar 1848, Benjamin Jones, adminr.

CONARD BREY, Upper Hanover, 2 Mar 1848, Charles Conard, Enos Conard, adminrs.

JESSE KENDERDINE, Moreland, 4 Mar 1848, Jane Kenderdine, adminr.

ELIZABETH HARLEY, Upper Providence, 7 Mar 1848, Catharine Harley, adminr.

DAVID RITTENHOUSE, Norriton, 15 Mar 1848, William Rittenhouse, Christopher Rittenhouse, Henry Rittenhouse, adminrs.

JACOB CUSTER, Limerick, 25 Mar 1848, Jacob Custer, adminr.

THOMAS HILBORN, Limerick, 27 Mar 1848, Jonathan Hilborn, James Hilborn, adminrs.

SUSANNA DAGER, Whitemarsh, 4 Apr 1848, John Dager, adminr.

JACOB CASSEL, Worcester, 5 Apr 1848, Charlotte Cassel, adminr.

JOSEPH TOMLINSON, Whitpain, 6 Apr 1848, Mary Tomlinson, Evan Davis, adminrs.

DANIEL HITTELL, Upper Hanover, 11 Apr 1848, John Hittell, John Fox, adminrs.

RACHEL BARLOW, Pottsgrove, 11 Apr 1848, Joel Harlow, Abraham Yorge, adminrs.

JAMES MAGEE, Horsham, 11 Apr 1848, Paul Dowlin, adminr.

ELIZABETH MILLER, Norristown, 19 Apr 1848, Daniel Miller, adminr.

FRANKLIN MCGLATHERY, Plymouth, 20 Apr 1848, Elizabeth McGlathery, adminr.

STEPHEN DOOD, Montgomery, 22 Apr 1848, Sarah Dood, adminr.

HEPSEY MCCANN, Norriton, 22 Apr 1848, William McCann, adminr.

ELIZABETH BITTING, Frederick, 24 Apr 1848, Jonathan Nyce, adminr.

WILLIAM TYSON, Worcester, 25 Apr 1848, Daniel Tyson, Samuel Tyson, adminrs.

GEORGE THOMAS, Norristown, 25 Apr 1848, Gilbert McCoy, adminr.

WILLIAM HORTON, Upper Merion, 28 Apr 1848, William Crombie, adminr.

ANNA DENGLER, Douglass, 2 May 1848, John Dengler, adminr.

ISAAC DEWEES, Plymouth, 9 May 1848, John Snyder, adminr.

JANE DAWSON, Montgomery, 11 May 1848, James Dawson, adminr.

WILLIAM WEBB, Norriton, 12 May 1848, William McCann, adminr.

ISAIAH KIMBEL, Abington, 15 May 1848, Maria Kimbel, George Kimbel, John Byerly, adminrs.

ABRAHAM ALLABACH, Towamencin, 15 May 1848, Amos Allabach, Jesse Allabach, adminrs.

JOHN GROB, Frederick, 16 May 1848, Mary Grob, adminr.

CATHARINE JONES, Frederick, 17 May 1848, Isaac Rahn, adminr.

ALEXANDER MCCOLLOM, Upper Merion, 19 May 1848, John McCoy, adminr.

DAVID HENDERSON, Upper Merion, 23 May 1848, Margaret Henderson, George Henderson, Samuel Henderson, adminrs.

DAVID KRIEBEL, Worcester, 25 May 1848, Jacob Kriebel, Jacob Anders, adminrs.

BENJAMIN BEAN, Skippack & Perkiomen, 30 May 1848, Susanna Bean, adminr.

ELIZABETH ROSEN, Lower Providence, 5 Jun 1848, Isaac Rosen, adminr.

JAMES O'NEIL, Norristown, 6 Jun 1848, H.B. Hancock, adminr.

JOHN GEORGE, Upper Hanover, 7 Jun 1848, Henry Jacob, adminr.

SUSANNA SCHULTZ, Worcester, 9 Jun 1848, Melchior Kriebel, William Kriebel, adminrs.

PATRICK COBEY, Pottstown, 8 Jun 1848, Thomas Cobey, adminr.

HANNAH KEELEY, Skippack & Perkiomen, 22 Jun 1848, William Keeley, adminr.

CHARLES STOUT, Upper Dublin, 22 Jun 1848, John Martin, adminr.

JONATHAN SHOEMAKER, Moreland, 24 Jun 1848, Hannah Shoemaker, Jonathan Lukens, adminrs.

JOEL BANES, Montgomery, 26 Jun 1848, Euphemia Banes, adminr.

DANIEL BOORSE, Towamencin, 14 Jul 1848, Abraham Hackman, Jacob Ruth, adminrs.

GARRET ZEIGLER, Lower Salford, 22 Jul 1848, Abraham Zeigler, Henry Bean, Henry Kolb, Gotshall Bergey, adminrs.

MATILDA TYSON, Abington, 22 Jul 1848, Edwin Tyson, adminr.

JOHN FRICK, Hatfield, 29 Jul 1848, Peter Frick, John Frick, adminrs.

WILLIAM YOUNG, Lower Providence, 31 Jul 1848, George Yost, adminrs.

LEONARD STREEPER, Springfield, 1 Aug 1848, Henry Streeper, Peter Streeper, David Streeper, adminrs.

SARAH JOHNSON, Upper Providence, 8 Aug 1848, Addison May, adminr.

ARNOLD BOYER, Skippack & Perkiomen, 9 Aug 1848, Joshua Heebner, adminr.

JACOB COLFLESH, Lower Merion, 10 Aug 1848, William Colflesh, adminr.

MARY TEANEY, Whitpain, 14 Aug 1848, Philip Gerhart, adminr.

MARY DILLION, Abington, 18 Aug 1848, Ardemus Steward, adminr.

SIMON ADAM, Upper Hanover, 21 Aug 1848, Simon Adam, John Adam, adminrs.

JOHN WICK, Frederick, 28 Aug 1848, Aaron Schwenk, adminr.

DANIEL FEGLEY, Douglass, 22 Aug 1848, John Fegley, Henry Buchard, adminrs.

JOHN STONG, Worcester, 22 Aug 1848, Henry Stong, Philip Stong, adminrs.

MARY BEANS, Upper Dublin, 23 Aug 1848, Edward Beans, adminr.

DANIEL STRAIN, Upper Merion, 26 Aug 1848, Bridget Strain, adminr.

JOHN GEHMAN, Hatfield, 29 Aug 1848, Jacob Gehman, Benjamin Rosenberger, adminrs.

ISAAC KENDERDINE, 7 Sep 1848, Sarah Kenderdine, Chalky Kenderdine, adminrs.

MARY MILLER New Hanover, 8 Sep 1848, Peter Miller, adminr.

JOHN ETTINGER, New Hanover, 15 Sep 1848, James Ettinger, adminr.

ABRAHAM DRACE, New Hanover, 22 Sep 1848, Michael Drace, Reuben Drace, adminrs.

HANNAH HUNSBERGER, Franconia, 29 Sep 1848, Jonathan Hunsberger, adminr.

DAVID DERRICKS, Lower Providence, 3 Oct 1848, Nathan Derricks, James Casselberry, adminrs.

MARGARET FLECK, Gwynedd, 9 Oct 1848, Susanna Bisbing, Joseph Bisbing, adminrs.

AARON SMITH, Lower Merion, 11 Oct 1848, Mary Smith, William Smith, adminrs.

HILRY SENN, Hatfield, 11 Oct 1848, Isaac Hunsberger, adminr.

GEORGE YEAKEL, Upper Hanover, 14 Oct 1848, Susanna Yeakel, adminr.

ANDREW YEAKEL, Upper Hanover, 14 Oct 1848, Susanna Yeakel, adminr.

JOHN CRATER, Perkiomen, 16 Oct 1848, Levi Crater, Abraham Funk, adminrs.

ABRAHAM YOST, Whitpain, 16 Oct 1848, Sarah Yost, adminr.

ABRAHAM JOHNSON, Upper Providence, 17 Oct 1848, Elizabeth Johnson, Jacob Johnson, adminrs.

JOHN KOCH, New Hanover, 18 Oct 1848, William Kepner, Henry Kolb, adminrs.

ABRAHAM YERKES, Whitemarsh, 18 Oct 1848, Silas Shoemaker, adminr.

WILLIAM CLAYTON, Moreland, 26 Oct 1848, George Shelmire, adminr.

ESTHER HERMAN, Norristown, 30 Oct 1848, William Schall, adminr.

JOHN RUTHERFORD, Moreland, 14 Nov 1848, Joseph Rutherford, adminr.

GEORGE GORDON, Horsham, 15 Nov 1848, George Gordon, adminr.

ANDREW LONG, Norristown, 18 Nov 1848, John Long, adminr.

JOHN MITCHELL, Lower Merion, 20 Nov 1848, Davis Mitchell, William Davis, adminrs.

HENRY GARBER, Upper Providence, 8 Dec 1848, Charles Garber, Theodore Garber, adminrs.

JACOB SLOUGH, Worcester, 9 Dec 1848, Jesse Horning, adminr.

SARAH SEYLOR, Upper Providence, 11 Dec 1848, John Spare, adminr.

EDWARD STACKER, Upper Merion, 15 Dec 1848, Joel Jones, adminr.

JACOB ERB, Frederick, 26 Dec 1848, William Specht, adminr.

SARAH SCHEETZ, Norriton, 28 Dec 1848, Matthias H. Scheetz, adminr.

JACOB GERHART, Upper Providence, 1 Jan 1849, Jacob Gerhart, adminr.

JESSE GAUGLER, Frederick, 18 Jan 1849, William Gaugler, adminr.

JACOB SEAHOLTZ, Upper Hanover, 26 Jan 1849, Charles Seaholtz, adminr.

GEORGE JONES, Horsham, 26 Jan 1849, William McClean, adminr.

GARRET GODSHALK, Towamencin, 2 Feb 1849, Benjamin Godshalk, Jones Godshalk, adminrs.

DAVID HARRY, Whitemarsh, 3 Feb 1849, Benjamin Harry, John Wood adminrs.

WILLIAM TWINING, Norristown, 5 Feb 1849, Lucretia Twining, Abishai Woodman, adminrs.

JOSHUA WALTON, Cheltenham, 10 Feb 1849, Isaac Walton, adminrs.

ISAAC DE HAVEN, Whitemarsh, 10 Feb 1849, Daniel Hitner, adminr.

JESSE DANEHOWER, Marlborough, 14 Feb 1849, Elizabeth Danehower, adminr.

JACOB SCHWEINHART, Douglass, 19 Feb 1849, Frederick Fegely, adminr.

MARY HARLEY, Lower Salford, 19 Feb 1849, William Harley, adminr.

JACOB PRINCE, Whitpain, 22 Feb 1849, Emanuel Wentz, adminr.

JOHN JONES, Whitemarsh, 28 Feb 1849, Mark Jones, adminr.

SAMUEL JOHNSON, Gwynedd, 2 Mar 1849, Abraham Danehower, Jacob Pruner, adminrs.

HARMAN LEWIS, Towamencin, Mar 1849, Peter Nyce, Lydia Lewis, adminrs.

MARGARET LARE, Norristown, 13 Mar 1849, Benjamin Powell, adminr.

JOHN LIGHTCAP, Norristown, 15 Mar 1849, George Lightcap, adminr.

MARK SWARK, Upper Salford, 23 Mar 1849, Charles Swark, adminr.

THOMAS PEIRCE, Whitemarsh, 24 Mar 1849, James Peirce, adminr.

SARAH FRY, Lower Merion, 24 Mar 1849, Levi Morris, adminr.

JACOB HALLMAN, Plymouth, 26 Mar 1849, Jacob Hallman, adminr.

FRANCIA LANDIS, Skippack & Perkiomen, 30 Mar 1849, Isaac Landis, adminr.

MARY KEELEY, Skippack & Perkiomen, 31 Mar 1849, Benjamin Keeley, adminr.

HENRY MOYER, Limerick, 3 Apr 1849, Samuel Moyer, Peter Saylor, adminrs.

ISABELLA KNOX, Norriton, 3 Apr 1849, Rebecca Knox, adminr.

PRISCILLA KENDERDINE, Horsham, 4 Apr 1849, Isaac Kenderdine, adminr.

GEORGE LUKENS, Towamencin, 9 Apr 1849, Esther Lukens, Abel Lukens, Seth Lukens, adminr.

JACOB RENNINGER, New Hanover, 11 Apr 1849, Henry Schneider, adminr.

FRANCIA O'KANE, Norristown, 19 Apr 1849, James O'Kane, adminr.

JAMES WHARTENLY, Abington, 21 Apr 1849, John McNair, adminr.

MORDECAI DAVIS, Towamencin, 30 Apr 1849, Edith Davis, adminr.

THOMAS FORD, Montgomery, 8 May 1849, William Ford, adminr.

BENJAMIN BARNES, Horsham, 21 May 1849, George Barnes, Joseph Stemple, adminrs.

DAVID YERKES, Moreland, 21 May 1849, Samuel Lukens, adminr.

RACHEL EVANS, Limerick, 22 May 1849, David Evans, adminr.

SARAH TEARY, Lower Providence, 22 May 1849, John Teary, adminr.

MARGARET HARWOOD, Worcester, 24 May 1849, John Roberts, adminr.

JAMES SPENCER, Upper Dublin, 24 May 1849, Spencer Shoemaker, adminr.

REGINA SCIPT, Towamencin, 1 Jun 1849, Abraham Scipt, Jacob Anders, adminrs.

ELIZABETH SCIPT, Towamencin, 1 Jun 1849, Abraham Scipt, Jacob Anders, adminrs.

KESIAH HENDERSON, Upper Merion, 9 Jun 1849, Samuel Traquau, adminr.

JOSEPH HALLMAN, Plymouth, 13 Jun 1849, John Hallman, adminr.

ANNA ROBERTS, Gwynedd, 25 Jun 1849, Isaac Wampole, adminr.

HENRY FISHER, Upper Dublin, 29 Jun 1849, Jacob Fisher, adminr.

MARY KNIPE, Montgomery, 3 Jul 1849, George Solladay, adminr.

WILLIAM LIVEZEY, Abington, 3 Jul 1849, Sarah Livezey, George Hiller, adminrs.

MICHAEL CASSEL, Worcester, 3 Jul 1849, Catharine Cassel, adminr.

GEORGE POTTS, Montgomery, 5 Jul 1849, John Stong, adminr.

SARAH FISHER, Upper Dublin, 6 Jul 1849, Jacob Fisher, adminr.

ABRAHAM WARNER, Norristown, 10 Jul 1849, Jacob Longaker, adminr.

HENRY BODEY, Whitemarsh, 16 Jul 1849, John Bodey, Jacob Bodey, Samuel Bodey, adminrs.

SARAH HENDRICKS, Pottsgrove, 21 Jul 1849, Aaron Linderman, John Christman, adminrs.

SUSANNA ENGLE, Douglass, 6 Aug 1849, John Engle, adminr.

WILLIAM HALLOWELL, Moreland, 10 Aug 1849, Margaret Hallowell, adminr.

JONATHAN SHOEMAKER, Moreland, 11 Aug 1849, Isaac Shoemaker, adminr.

MARY LANDIS, Skippack & Perkiomen, 13 Aug 1849, William Fox, adminr.

MICHAEL DANEHOWER, Upper Merion, 30 Aug 1849, Thomas Dunn, adminr.

ISAAC WITCOMB, Upper Dublin, 14 Aug 1849, Catharine Witcomb, adminr.

ANDREW KEIGER, Upper Merion, 18 Aug 1849, William Keiger, Colbert Keiger, adminr.

DAVID BURKETT, Douglass, 20 Aug 1849, Hetty Burkett, William Mack, adminrs.

DAVID SANDERS, Gwynedd, 3 Nov 1849, John Shaneberger, adminr.

JOHN DAVIS, Hatfield, 7 Nov 1849, Joel Davis, Septimus Evans, Enos Matthias, adminrs.

MARGARET DAVIS, Upper Merion, 8 Nov 1849, James Shock, adminr.

HENRY KOHL, Limerick, 10 Nov 1849, Abraham Kohl, Sebastian Kohl, Joseph Kohl, adminrs.

DANIEL SMITH, New Hanover, 19 Nov 1849, Hetty Smith, Henry Harple, adminrs.

MARTIN LEAPSON, Cheltenham, 19 Nov 1849, Thomas Page, Rowland Page, Christian Page, adminr.

ABRAHAM LUKENS, Moreland, 21 Nov 1849, Lemen Panes, adminr.

JOHN PRAYER, Lower Merion, 4 Dec 1849, John Prayer, adminr.

AQUILLA TOOL, Upper Dublin, 6 Dec 1849, Stephen Tool, adminr.

JOHN WHITE, Plymouth, 6 Dec 1849, Jacob White, adminr.

ZEBEDA DORN, Moreland, 8 Dec 1849, Ellwood Dorn, adminr.

CATHARINE SAYLOR, Pottstown, 8 Dec 1849, Godfrey Saylor, adminr.

WILLIAM MARPOLE, Plymouth, 10 Dec 1849, Enoch Marpole, adminr.

REBECCA WENTZ, Upper Merion, 11 Dec 1849, Samuel Phillips, adminr.

DANIEL NACE, Whitemarsh, 13 Dec 1849, Maria Nace, adminr.

MAGDALENA DE HAVEN, Whitpain, 15 Dec 1849, David De Haven, adminr.

WILLIAM BROADES, Lower Merion, 17 Dec 1849, Richard Broades, adminr.

DAVID WILKINS, Upper Providence, 18 Dec 1849.

THOMAS HORNMILLER, Moreland, 19 Dec 1849, John Smith, adminr.

WILLIAM CHITTLE, Montgomery, 27 Dec 1849, John Brown, adminr.

MARY KOLB, Springfield, 28 Dec 1849, Daniel Kolb, adminr.

AMOS JONES, Pottstown, 28 Dec 1849, Jonas Smith, adminr.

JOHN SMITH, Pottstown, 29 Dec 1849, Amelia Smith, adminr.

JOHN SHADE, Upper Providence, 2 Jan 1850, Uriah Shade, adminr.

WILLIAM ENGLE, Gwynedd, 5 Jan 1850, B.F. Taylor, adminr.

JOHN REITER, Marlborough, 8 Jan 1850, James Reiter, Franklin Reiter, adminrs.

ISAAC BURK, Upper Dublin, 15 Jan 1850, Charles Burk, adminr.

ANN HARNER, Upper Dublin, 15 Jan 1850, George Wilson, adminr.

CATHARINE COPE, Gwynedd, 18 Jan 1850, Abraham Danehower, adminr.

JACOB LEISLER, Marlborough, 21 Jan 1850, Franklin Leisler, adminr.

WILLIAM PRICE, Lower Salford, 28 Jan 1850, Timothy Price, adminr.

MARY BRIGGS, Norristown, 6 Feb 1850, Alfred Briggs, adminr.

MARY WALTERS, Whitpain, 9 Feb 1850, Samuel Walters, adminr.

SAMUEL LEIDIG, Frederick, 9 Feb 1850, Samuel Roeller, George Poley, adminrs.

ANDREW SLICK, Frederick, 9 Feb 1850, Benjamin Johnson, adminr.

LYDIA CRATER, Frederick, 18 Feb 1850, Aaron Schwenk, adminr.

CHRISTIAN SCHWENKHARD, Douglass, 19 Feb 1850, William Mock, adminr.

ISAAC WALTON, Upper Merion, 25 Feb 1850, Mary Walton, adminr.

HENRY MASSEY, Moreland, 7 Mar 1850, Silas Yerkes, adminr.

JOHN BEAN, Skippack & Perkiomen, 7 Mar 1850, Joseph Bean, Isaac Bean, adminrs.

DANIEL SCHLICHTER, Upper Hanover, 7 Mar 1850, George Slichter, adminr.

REBECCA STOGDALE, Moreland, 12 Mar 1850, John Smith, adminr.

JOHN DAVIS, Upper Dublin, 15 Mar 1850, John Gamble, adminr.

JOSEPH ABRAHAM, Upper Merion, 29 Mar 1850, James Abraham, Benjamin Abraham, adminrs.

THOMAS CASON, Norriton, 3 Apr 1850, John Cason, adminr.

DENNIS COURREN, Norristown, 4 Apr 1850, Bridget Courren, adminr.

HENRY STOUT, Cheltenham, 4 Apr 1850, Christian Stout, adminr.

JOHN OTTINGER, Springfield, 4 Apr 1850, Daniel Fisher, adminr.

JACOB HILDEBIDLE, Upper Providence, 11 Apr 1850, John Hildebidle, John Dismant, adminrs.

DILLMAN KOLB, Skippack & Perkiomen, 12 Apr 1850, Isaac Kolb, adminr.

LEONARD KOLB, 13 Apr 1850, Daniel Kolb, adminr.

HENRY KOLB, Lower Salford, 16 Apr 1850, William Kolb, adminr.

ELIZABETH KOONS, Frederick, 19 Apr 1850, Samuel Koons, adminr.

MARIA URFFER, Upper Hanover, 22 Apr 1850, Philip Super, adminr.

JOSEPH UMSTEAD, Lower Providence, 23 Apr 1850, Susanna Umstead, adminr.

CHRISTIAN DETWILER, 30 Apr 1850, Catharine Detwiler, Samuel Rosenberger, adminrs.

JAMES PAUL, Abington, 30 Apr 1850, Israel Walton, adminr.

SARAH HOOVEN, Upper Dublin, 30 May 1850, Charles Hooven, adminr.

JOHN HULDERMAN, Upper Salford, 31 May 1850, Joseph Hulderman, adminr.

ISRAEL HOXWORTH, Lower Providence, 4 Jun 1850, Mary Hoxworth, Edward Hoxworth, adminrs.

MICHAEL QUINLAN, Norristown, 5 Jun 1850, Clementine Quinlan, adminr.

SILAS JONES, Lower Merion, 7 Jun 1850, Nathan Jones, adminr.

HENRY PENNEBECKER, New Hanover, 7 Jun 1850, Elizabeth, Pennebecker, adminr.

SOPHIA UMSTEAD, 10 Jun 1850, Daniel Fry, adminr.

SOPHIA UMSTEAD, Upper Providence, 11 Jun 1850, John Miller, adminr.

CHARLES JOHNSON, Abington, 14 Jun 1850, Nathaniel Johnson, adminr.

GEORGE HURST, Whitpain, 15 Jun 1850, Jonathan Baker, adminr.

JOHN BRANDT, Franconia, 15 Jun 1850, Sophia Brand, Charles Frederick, adminrs.

EDWARD HOXWORTH, Hatfield, 20 Jun 1850, B.F. Hancock, adminr.

JOHN HEEBNER, Lower Providence, 17 Jun 1850, Christopher Heebner, adminr.

ALBERT MANUEL, Hatfield, 21 Jun 1850, Ann Manuel, John Evans, adminrs.

JACOB ZOLLER, Pottstown, 26 Jun 1850, Esther Zoller, adminr.

JAMES DUNCAN, Franconia, 8 Jul 1850, Isaac Wetherill, adminr.

CATHARINE BRANDT, Franconia, 8 Jul 1850, Charles Frederick, adminr.

SPENCER THOMAS, Upper Dublin, 15 Jul 1850, Samuel Lukens, Thomas Lukens, Algernon Lukens, adminrs.

JOHN PRIZER, Upper Providence, 17 Jul 1850, Frederick Prizer, John Prizer, adminrs.

JACOB GERHART, Franconia, 22 Jul 1850, Jacob Gerhart, Joseph Gerhart, adminrs.

JACOB BRUNNER, Limerick, 31 Jul 1850, William Bean, Thomas Rambo, adminrs.

ELIZABETH WEBER, Worcester, 12 Aug 1850, John Weber, adminr.

JOHN HEIST, Marlborough, 14 Aug 1850, Simon Hauck, adminr.

EVERHART KLINGER, 19 Aug 1850, Henry Essig, adminr.

JOHN SMITH, New Hanover, 20 Aug 1850, Reuben Steltz, adminr.

GEORGE LEHMAN, Worcester, 20 Aug 1850, Hannah Lehman, adminr.

ABRAHAM YERGEY, Pottstown, 20 Aug 1850, Sarah Yergey, adminr.

ELIAS JONES, Whitpain, 27 Aug 1850, Elizabeth Jones, adminr.

GEORGE WHITE, Plymouth, 30 Aug 1850, Daniel Kolp, adminr.

MARY DANEHOWER, Upper Dublin, 31 Aug 1850, Thomas Danehower, adminr.

BENJAMIN KEYSER, Worcester, 2 Sep 1850, John Keyser, adminr.

RACHEL RITTENHOUSE, Norristown, 3 Sep 1850, William Rittenhouse, adminr.

MARGARET MAXWELL, Lower Merion, 16 Sep 1850, Joseph Jones, adminr.

NORRIS JONES, Upper Dublin, 19 Sep 1850, Hannah Jones, Thomas Jones, adminrs.

MARY ORTLIP, Pottsgrove, 25 Sep 1850, John Ortlip, adminr.

WILLIAM DUNN, Lower Merion, 27 Sep 1850, George Smith, adminr.

LYDIA DAVIS, Lower Merion, 27 Sep 1850, Mark Bartleson, adminr.

REUBEN BOORSE, 7 Oct 1850, Jonas Boorse, adminr.

BENJAMIN MCLEVAN, 11 Oct 1850, Reiannah LeVan, adminr.

DANIEL WALT, Upper Providence, 14 Oct 1850, Jacob Walt, John Rambo, adminrs.

GEORGE WELKER, Upper Hanover, 14 Oct 1850, Isaac Welker, Samuel Welker, adminrs.

HENRY SWARTLEY, Skippack & Perkiomen, 17 Oct 1850, Francis Poley, adminr.

ALFRED DAVIS, Norristown, 21 Oct 1850, Joshua Davis, adminr.

JOHN BISSON, Gwynedd, 21 Oct 1850, Leah Bisson, Algernon Jenkins, adminrs.

CHARLES PENNEBECKER, New Hanover, 29 Oct 1950, Hannah Pennebecker, Philip Gable, adminrs.

JAMES FARMER, Plymouth 30 Oct 1850, John Ramsey, adminr.

TOBIAS HETRICK, Franconia, 31 Oct 1850, Elizabeth Hetrick, adminr.

WILLIAM SUPPLEE, Upper Merion, 31 Oct 1850, Joseph Jarrett, John Supplee, adminrs.

ABRAHAM MILLER, Upper Providence, 5 Nov 1850, Daniel Fry, adminr.

CHARLES HEIST, Moreland, 18 Nov 1850, David Heist, adminr.

JACOB YOCUM, Pottsgrove, 18 Nov 1850, Jonas Yocum, Aaron Yocum, adminrs.

PETER HOXWORTH, Hatfield, 18 Nov 1850, Sarah Hoxworth, John Hoxworth, adminrs.

SOPHIA BARNHART, New Hanover, 18 Nov 1850, William Specht, adminr.

WILLIAM JOHNSON, Upper Providence, 19 Nov 1850, Benjamin Johnson, adminr.

HANNAH EVANS, Limerick, 27 Nov 1850, Jesse Evans, adminr.

LYDIA ELLIS, Gwynedd, 30 Nov 1850, Isaac Ellis, adminr.

JOHN DAVIS, Towamencin, 9 Dec 1850, John Sterigere, adminr.

SOLOMON MISSIMER, Limerick, 10 Dec 1850, Maria Missimer, Jacob Missimer, adminrs.

ELIZABETH TRANBOWER, Lower Salford, 26 Dec 1850, James Weireman, adminr.

JONATHAN IREDELL, Horsham, 28 Dec 1850, Robert Iredell, adminr.

JOSEPH FREED, Franconia, 28 Dec 1850, Isaac Freed, John Freed, adminrs.

CHARLES EDLEMAN, Marlborough, 28 Dec 1850, Ruphina Edleman, adminr.

MARK KEELEY, Whitemarsh, 29 Aug 1850, Samuel Keeley, adminr.

ABRAHAM WEIRMAN, 20 Aug 1849, John Weirman, Benjamin Rosenberger, adminrs.

JOHN BELGER, Marlborough, 21 Aug 1849, Joseph Quicley, adminr.

MATTHEW WITCOMB, Upper Dublin, 21 Aug 1849, Frederick Nash, adminr.

JOSEPH CLOUD, Norristown, 22 Aug 1849, Elizabeth Cloud, adminr.

ANNA HARRY, Whitemarsh, 22 Aug 1849, Benjamin Harry, adminr.

SAMUEL POTTS, Lower Merion, 25 Aug 1849, John Newberry, adminr.

THOMAS HEALE, Upper Merion, 27 Aug 1849, Robert Heale, adminr.

MARY RENNINGER, Upper Hanover, 27 Aug 1849, William Specht, adminr.

PETER HENDRICKS, New Hanover, 29 Aug 1849, Isaac Geist, adminr.

PETER RITTENHOUSE, Springfield, 30 Aug 1849, George Rittenhouse, adminr.

FREDERICK DECKER, Upper Dublin, 30 Aug 1849, George Rittenhouse, adminr.

HENRY CASSEL, Skippack & Perkiomen, 3 Sep 1849, Jacob Cassel, adminr.

HENRY KINSEY, Lower Salford, 8 Sep 1849, Jacob Kinsey, John Kinsey, adminrs.

JOSEPH FITZGERALD, Whitpain, 10 Sep 1849, John Fitzgerald, adminr.

CHRISTIAN STOEVER, Worcester, 13 Sep 1849, Eli Stoever, Abraham Hendricks, adminr.

JOHN GEORGE KEILER, Pottsgrove, 15 Sep 1849, George Keiler, adminr.

ALEXANDER MCMULLEN, Lower Providence, 21 Sep 1849, William McMullen, adminr.

JOHN KEILER, Pottsgrove, 2 Oct 1849, Peter Keiler, John Keiler, adminrs.

ELIZABETH MORGAN, Whitpain, 4 Oct 1849, Morgan Morgan, adminr.

RACHEL FREAS, Whitemarsh, 6 Oct 1849, John Freas, Samuel Lightcap, adminrs.

SUSANNA SPRINGER, Towamencin, 6 Oct 1849, Levi Springer, adminr.

GEORGE WALT, Limerick, 8 Oct 1849, Henry Walt, adminr.

JOHN JARRETT, Horsham, 10 Oct 1849, Jonathan Jarrett, William Jarrett, adminrs.

JOHN MISSIMER, Pottsgrove, 10 Oct 1849, Zenas Saverge, adminr.

ISAAC WELLS, Pottstown, 15 Oct 1849, Isaac Wells, adminr.

ISAAC SCHOLFIELD, Abington, 19 Oct 1849, Ellen Scholfield, adminr.

HENRY FETTER, Pottstown, 19 Oct 1849, Catharine Fetter, adminr.

SAMUEL ROSHONG, Frederick, 24 Oct 1849, Benjamin Schedel, adminr.

JEREMIAH MASTER, Upper Hanover, 27 Oct 1849, Jacob Master, adminr.

JOHN SHAY, Horsham, 2 Nov 1849, John Shay, Edward Shay, adminrs.

Heritage Books by Mary Marshall Brewer:

Abstracts of Administrations of Montgomery County, Pennsylvania, 1822–1850

Abstracts of Land Records of King George County, Virginia, 1752–1783

Abstracts of Land Records of Richmond County, Virginia, 1692–1704

Abstracts of the Wills of Montgomery County, Pennsylvania, 1824–1850

Early Union County, New Jersey Church Records, 1750–1800

Essex County, Virginia Land Records, 1752–1761

Essex County, Virginia Land Records 1761–1772

Essex County, Virginia Land Records 1772–1786

Kent County, Delaware Guardian Accounts: Aaron to Carty, 1752–1849

Kent County, Delaware Guardian Accounts: Caton to Edinfield, 1753–1849

Kent County, Delaware Guardian Accounts: Edmondson to Hopkins, 1744–1855

Kent County, Delaware Guardian Accounts: Houston to McBride, 1739–1856

Kent County, Delaware Guardian Accounts: McBride to Savin, 1739–1851

Kent County, Delaware Guardian Accounts: Savin to Truax, 1754–1852

Kent County, Delaware Guardian Accounts: Truitt to Young, 1755–1849

Kent County, Delaware Land Records, 1776–1783

Kent County, Delaware Land Records, 1782–1785

Kent County, Delaware Land Records, 1785–1789

Kent County, Delaware Land Records, 1788–1792

King George County, Virginia Court Orders, 1746–1751

King George County, Virginia Court Orders, 1751–1754

Land Records of Sussex County, Delaware, 1681–1725

Land Records of Sussex County, Delaware, 1753–1763

Land Records of Sussex County, Delaware, 1763–1769

Land Records of Sussex County, Delaware: Various Dates: 1693–1698, 1715–1717, 1782–1792, 1802–1805

Land Records of York County, Pennsylvania, Libers A and B, 1746–1764

Land Records of York County, Pennsylvania, Libers C and D, 1764–1771

Land Records of York County, Pennsylvania, Libers E and F, 1771–1775

Land Records of York County, Pennsylvania, Libers G and H, 1775–1793

New Castle County, Delaware Wills, 1800–1813

Northumberland County, Virginia: Deeds, Wills, Inventories, etc., 1737–1743

Northumberland County, Virginia: Deeds, Wills, Inventories, etc., 1743–1749

Probate Records of Kent County, Delaware, Volume 1: 1801–1812

Probate Records of Kent County, Delaware, Volume 2: 1812–1822

Probate Records of Kent County, Delaware, Volume 3: 1822–1833

Quaker Records of Cedar Creek Monthly Meeting: Virginia, 1739–1793

Spotsylvania County, Virginia Deed Books, 1722–1734

Spotsylvania County, Virginia Deed Books, 1734–1751

York County, Virginia Deeds, Orders, Wills, Etc., 1698–1700

York County, Virginia Deeds, Orders, Wills, Etc., 1700–1702

York County, Virginia Deeds, Orders, Wills, Etc., 1705–1706

York County, Virginia Deeds, Orders, Wills, Etc., 1714–1716

York County, Virginia Deeds, Orders, Wills, Etc., 1716–1718

York County, Virginia Deeds, Orders, Wills, Etc., 1718–1720

York County, Virginia Deeds, Orders, Wills, Etc., 1728–1732

York County, Virginia Land Records: 1694–1713

York County, Virginia Land Records:1713–1729

York County, Virginia Land Records: 1729–1763

York County, Virginia Land Records: 1763–1777

York County, Virginia Wills, Inventories and Court Orders, 1702–1704

York County, Virginia Wills, Inventories and Court Orders, 1732–1737

York County, Virginia Wills, Inventories and Court Orders, 1737–1740

York County, Virginia Wills, Inventories and Court Orders, 1740–1743

York County, Virginia Wills, Inventories and Court Orders, 1743–1746

York County, Virginia Wills, Inventories and Court Orders, 1745–1759

www.ingramcontent.com/pod-product-compliance
Lightning Source LLC
Chambersburg PA
CBHW070921270326
41927CB00011B/2674
* 9 7 8 1 6 8 0 3 4 9 4 5 0 *